Stephan van Erp, André Lascaris (Eds)

Who is Afraid of Postmodernism?

RELIGION – GESCHICHTE – GESELLSCHAFT
Fundamentaltheologische Studien

herausgegeben von

Johann Baptist Metz (Münster/Wien)
Johann Reikerstorfer (Wien)
Jürgen Werbick (Münster)

Band 38

LIT

Stephan van Erp, André Lascaris (Eds)

Who is Afraid of Postmodernism?

Challenging Theology for a Society in Search of Identity

With a Preface by Robert J. Schreiter

LIT

Gedruckt auf alterungsbeständigem Werkdruckpapier entsprechend
ANSI Z3948 DIN ISO 9706

Bibliographic information published by Die Deutsche Bibliothek
Die Deutsche Bibliothek lists this publication in the Deutsche
Nationalbibliografie; detailed bibliographic data are available in the
Internet at http://dnb.ddb.de.

ISBN 3-8258-8781-2

A catalogue record for this book is available from the British Library

© LIT VERLAG Münster   2005
Grevener Str./Fresnostr. 2   D- 48159 Münster
Tel. +49/(0)251-620320   Fax +49/(0)251-23 19 72
e-Mail: lit@lit-verlag.de   http://www.lit-verlag.de

Distributed in the UK by: Global Book Marketing, 38 King Street, London WC 2E 8JT
Phone: +44 (0) 207 240 6649 – Fax: +44 (0) 20 7497 0309, http://www.globalbookmarketing.co.uk

Distributed in North America by:

Transaction Publishers
New Brunswick (U.S.A.) and London (U.K.)

Transaction Publishers   Tel.: (732) 445 - 2280
Rutgers University   Fax: (732) 445 - 3138
35 Berrue Circle   for orders (U. S. only):
Piscataway, NJ 08854   toll free (888) 999 - 6778

Table of Contents

Preface
by ROBERT J. SCHREITER   7

STEPHAN VAN ERP AND ANDRÉ LASCARIS
Introduction   11

ANDRÉ LASCARIS
Can I Say 'We'?
*An Encounter Between the Good Samaritan and
Three Postmodern Philosophers*   16

ERIK BORGMAN
Alienation as Identity
Believing in Cultivated Vulnerability   34

MANUELA KALSKY
Through the Eyes of the Other
Towards a Feminist Revision of Christology   46

AD WILLEMS
The Greatness of a Little Narrative
Reflection on a Powerless Christian Identity   64

ANNE-CLAIRE MULDER AND LEO OOSTERVEEN
Landing Stages for the Divine
A Correspondence on Transcendence and Everyday Life   80

List of Contributors   116

Preface

The Postmodern comes to us in many forms. This no doubt reflects the "post" prefix on the word itself: we have a good idea what modernity is, and we know that we are now in something new and different. Yet we still cannot give it clearer definition. There is a lack of certainty about how to approach it, yet there are two discernible points where varieties of the postmodern cluster.

One point, around which a number of views coalesce, might equally well be called "countermodern" or even "antimodern." This point of view gathers together movements and ideas that find fault with the direction modernity has taken. More specifically, they react against what Muslim scholar Bassam Tibi has called "cultural modernity" (as opposed to "institutional modernity"– that is, the modernity brought about by the natural sciences and technology). Cultural modernity, he tells us, is based on the principle of the individual subject, free to determine his or her own path through life, and free as well to change the natural and social environment. The various fundamentalisms found in religions and ideologies around the world reflect one form of turning away from cultural modernity. Although they may invoke an idealized premodern past, they use modern and postmodern means to communicate their views. There are however more moderate reactions against cultural modernity, that either invoke an idealized earlier time when life was more coherent and collective (as do the theologians of Radical Orthodoxy, who appeal to the European Middle Ages), or seek to burrow into a single linguistic-cultural community to recreate that sense of collective commitment (as do postliberal theologians). In all of these instances, the fragmentation of communities is seen as an outcome of modernity, and as something that has to be rejected and remedied.

The other pole gives witness to a more forthright struggle with the consequences of modernity, trying to create a humane life amid the fragments and ruptures, realizing that modernity cannot be turned back or be undone. Some have called this "hypermodernity" (as has Zygmunt Bauman) since it represents a heightened sense of the consequences of modernity. For others, this represents the quintessential postmodern stance. It recognizes that any response to the modern will remain in some fashion indebted to the modern – something some of the points of view clustering around the other pole do not appear to comprehend. How to negotiate the fragmentation, the seeming lack of tradition as any sort of guide, and the possibilities and the problems of the individual subject is a continuing quest.

This latter experience of the postmodern is most evident today in Europe, home and progenitor of modernity itself. It is especially salient in northern Europe, where one finds the highest levels of individualism and secularized societies. It is nearly as strong – especially among the youngest age cohorts – in North America and Australia and New Zealand. But it can be found nearly everywhere around the planet, especially among those who live with and within the communication technologies that are the infrastructure of globalization.

The postmodern challenges Christian faith in a dramatic way, since it appears to go against the very grain of a sense of tradition, communion, and commitment. Some Christians have sought refuge from postmodernity by trying to return to the "Age of Faith" (as does Radical Orthodoxy), while others create for themselves a distinctively antimodern reading of their own origins (as do fundamentalists). But there are others who feel that a genuinely Christian way to live in postmodernity can be found, just as earlier generations struggled to combine Christianity and modernity. Some things may be lost, but new possibilities are discovered as well.

This collection of essays, by a group of Dutch theologians who have set their purpose as one of finding faithful ways to live out Christianity in a secular, postmodern environment, will stimulate the imagination of anyone who reads them. The tone of the essays is one of searching and sometimes uncertainty – not uncertainty about the value of Christian faith, but uncertainty representing an honesty about the new pathways that need to be charted. The authors represent a range of age as well. Some were involved in the struggle to create a more open stance of Christians to modernity itself; others have come of age in the full tide of postmodernity. That they can and do engage in dialogue is the best proof of the validity of the path they are walking together: toward a faithful yet prophetic living of Christian faith in a very changed world.

It might seem odd that a collection of essays from the Netherlands is being published for an audience in the United States. But a closer reflection reveals how timely this is. The Netherlands is one of the most secularized countries in Europe – far more so than the United States. But its move into modernity and now postmodernity has occurred in just slightly more than a generation. The Dutch experience of this transition provides a look at the dynamic in foreshortened form, thereby instructive for others. It will help chart the way ahead for how postmodernity will continue to develop on this side of the Atlantic Ocean. There has also been a long affinity between the Netherlands and the United States as well. The Dutch were the first religiously tolerant country in Europe, giving safe haven to the Pilgrims, whose stamp on American culture is still tangible today. The Netherlands signed the first amity pact with the United States of any European country. And the two countries share values such as self-reliance, regard for initiative, and affirmation of the right to be different.

So I commend these essays to you. Essays are perhaps the best way to approach the postmodern. The dialogue (as found in the chapter which is an exchange of letters) is likewise particularly apt for this genre. My hope is that they will stimulate your thinking about the postmodern as they did mine.

Robert J. Schreiter

Introduction

Stephan van Erp and André Lascaris

Who is afraid of postmodernism? The authors of this book are not. To them, today's world is 'postmodern'. They see a fragmented world, in which ideologies and 'great narratives' seem to have lost their attraction. The fall of the Berlin wall and the collapse of the iron curtain put an end to the easy division of the world into a 'we' and a 'them'. Now that these easy distinctions are gone, people get disoriented. Some politicians may try to establish a new division between the so-called Christian and the Islamic worlds, but even if they manage to achieve this either purposefully or by chance, the world would still be a postmodern one. Other developments may be equally important for a different appreciation of today's reality.

While some walls fall down other walls may be put up. When postmodernism encourages people to develop a personal and individual lifestyle, it becomes implausible to have a public debate. One establishes the fact that other persons have a different view, think and act differently, but as long as this does not become an obstacle to 'my' lifestyle, discussing, debating or putting forward one's arguments become quite superfluous. Why have a debate if it is not possible to find a common point of view, a unity in purpose, truth? Being silent is dear to many postmodern philosophers and theologians.

In the second half of the twentieth century, the theological debate was intense. Theologians were busy catching up with modern thought and the ideals and hopes their contemporaries cherished. Once they had managed to meet the challenges of modern life, theologians found that new ones had replaced them already. For in the meantime, more and more people started questioning those modern ideals. High expectations that all of humanity would be united in a liberal and tolerant attitude have been shattered as a result. The idea that mankind is continually progressing towards a better future, crossing new frontiers all the time, the idea that society will evolve into a higher and more happy state of being, has become implausible. There are too many poor in today's world, too many people are second class citizens, and both men and women are oppressed or even persecuted because of their racial, religious, social or sexual identity. From the eighteenth century onwards, every new generation of 'modern people' considered reason to be the way to safety and security, and to put history on a firm footing. However, at the beginning of the 21st century, uncertainty holds sway. Reason, our crowning achievement, has been dethroned and driven into exile. Once, it made people resist political and religious authority and defend the uniqueness of the individual, but it became a power that colonized everything and turned authoritarian. The detrimental effects of modern technical genius now confront people with the danger of ecological disaster. Everybody is allowed to desire everything, and to try and get whatever he or she likes. This kind of freedom has made us all into rivals and competitors, and in the end, none of us are free anymore.

Postmodern philosophers offer a challenging analysis of the decay of the ideals of modernity. They show the necessity of a radical rethinking of the presuppositions and structures of modern thought. Do those structures allow room for the concrete, different life stories of individuals? Do the ideals of modern times gloss over social and cultural differences? Do they mould individuals into tools for the sake of emancipation? People will have to accept that the future is more indeterminate than they once believed. They will have to take risks, because life goes on and decisions have to be taken, and they will not be able to account for every aspect of their lives. They will have to act all the time, knowing that every solution to a problem creates another and often an unexpected one.

The authors of this book try to develop a critical theological view on postmodernism. They neither applaud nor lament postmodernism. They see it as a social and cultural context of which they are part, and ask (from different philosophical and theological perspectives) how we can think and speak theologically in a postmodern world. What should theology be like in a time in which great narratives that brought people together lose their appeal? What do theologians have to say? How can we commit ourselves to God, Church and religion in a time of such rapid changes that seems to make people want more than one identity? Moreover, as the churches in Europe seem to get emptier by the week, outside the religious institutions, religion flourishes in all kinds of forms. Rather than giving up the debate, the authors are continually in discussion with postmodern thinkers, with their Christian and theological background and with one another.

The authors of this book are all Europeans. For a long time, Americans who wanted to study theology often came to the old continent of Europe, while American theology was almost unknown in Europe. Over the last ten years, the positions reversed. America became an important source of theological thought for European theologians. European students are leaving for the United States to study theology. Hopefully, this book will help to bridge the ocean of not knowing between theology in the United States and Europe.

The contributions in this book were written by members or associated members of the Dominican Study Centre for Theology and Society in Nijmegen, the Netherlands, a small ecumenical group of women and men, financially supported by the Dutch branch of the Order of Preachers (Dominicans). The authors wrote their contributions on the basis of a series of discussions at the Study Centre. In the course of those discussions, each member of staff chose a point of departure from his or her personal and theological background.

How do people live together with other people in a postmodern culture, and how do they form a community? Am I allowed to use the word 'we' sometimes, or should I only use the word 'I'? Do people still develop a common identity? This is the theme of the first contribution in this book. The author, *André Lascaris*, is in discussion with postmodern philosophers like Richard Rorty, Jean-François Lyotard and Jacques Derrida. By interpreting the parable of the Good Samaritan from a postmodern point of view, he tries to develop a concept of a community that does not deprive individuals of their individuality.

How to start an attempt to build a community? *Ad Willems* begins his contribution by reporting on an experience of a 'limited' 'we': the celebration of the Eucharist in a student's chaplaincy in which God is experienced as silence. Both the traditional ideal of community building and the postmodern tendency to fragment communities become less important because of this experience. The author argues for a revaluation of the contemplative function of reason. This is necessary in order to be able to be open to the welcoming effect of the story of the other person. Only in such a context it is possible that people meet, and that sometimes 'Church' may take place.

Many people cherish nostalgia for a strong and self-confident community, as they existed in the past. In the 19th and the first half of the 20th century, religious leaders of the Catholic Church for instance, called on the faithful to shape their identity as a powerful resistance against modernity. Such a strong sense of identity is no longer possible after the horrifying events of the 20th century, of which Auschwitz is the symbol, and of the beginning of the 21st century, in which the fall of the Twin Towers undoubtedly marks the start of a new spate of violence. *Erik Borgman* assumes that identity always implies a moment of choice. Living in a postmodern culture entails uncertainty about one's identity, even if one feels part of a vulnerable community. With the American theologian Darrell Fasching, Borgman is convinced that after Auschwitz, Christians are forever strangers within their tradition that made those events possible. According to him, Christians can only find their identity in this alienation. Such an identity is vulnerable, but this weakness expresses openness to the desire for salvation.

The Christian community and identity are related to Christ. However, does the word 'Christ' mean the same for everybody, for both women and men, for western and non-western cultures? *Manuela Kalsky* shows that the discovery in feminist theology of the contextual differences among women has evoked postmodern questions from within. The 'great narrative' of Christology is criticized, and has to be rewritten under the pressure of the plurality of the 'little narratives' of women. According to her, the feminist theological revision of Christology has to go hand in hand with a drastic change of current epistemology. She uses the term 'christaphany', manifestation of Christa, to indicate the multitude of expectations and representations of salvation in different cultures. Christaphanies can therefore not be reduced to the logics of one christological system. The encounter with women from different cultures and their communication about contextual christaphanies is paramount, precisely to prevent the creation of new absolute and specific doctrinal systems of salvation. Moments of truth are to be found in the encounter with other types of experiences such as the everyday reality of women in different contexts. Rather than creating a synthesis of the various positions, the ongoing discussion of theologians with different points of view will break open the familiar epistemological habits and create new possibilities for an understanding of universality that is based on relations. The crossroads of these different personal experiences and their socio-political analysis expose the oppressive structures and open up the possibility for a new understanding of universality as an 'interactive universality'.

The final contribution has itself the form of a debate. It raises the question how postmodern people can imagine God. This contribution by *Leo Oosterveen* and *Anne-Claire Mulder* has a special structure: it consists of six letters they wrote to each other. In these letters, they share their thoughts on the role of transcendence in their every day life. They look back at their parting from the traditional images of God and try to find new names for the transcendent reality of the divine. Words such as 'light in one's existence' and 'source of life energy' emerge. Where to find this divine transcendence? Following in the footsteps of the medieval mystic Master Eckhart, the French feminist philosopher Luce Irigaray and the German philosopher Walter Benjamin, they point at the experience of the ultimate meaning of life, the materiality of the body and the role of the interrupting memory; these may be places where transcendence can now be encountered. Again and again, they return to the question how daily life can be shaped in such a way that there is room for the experience of transcendence. They do not pretend to provide a definite answer, but try to stimulate an ongoing discussion.

We are grateful to Professor Dennis Rochford, Head of the School of Theology of the Australian Catholic University, New South Wales, Australia, and to John Orme Mills, Cambridge, for their critical revision of the English translation, and to Professor Robert J. Schreiter, of the Catholic Theological Union of Chicago, U.S.A., for his advice, his encouragement and his willingness to write a preface to this book.

Can I Say 'We'?

An Encounter
Between the Good Samaritan and Three Postmodern Philosophers

André Lascaris

Introduction

My office is located on the seventeenth floor of an office block at the University of Nijmegen. This modern building could be anywhere, in any city, in the Netherlands or elsewhere. Modern buildings are typically built of steel, concrete and glass. They are huge but very evenly formed. The large expanses of glass suggest they have nothing to hide. On the inside they are exactly what you would expect them to be from the outside. They are open and democratic, that is, their design is clear and provides an insight to what is going on inside. They are meant for flexible use where spaces can be made bigger or smaller, with little effort, while the basic structure remains the same.

This is in stark contrast with the University of Oxford where I once studied. Some of the buildings in Oxford are of medieval origin. They were built with stone from local quarries. These have now been weathered, and restoration has to be performed with stone that must be imported from a specific area in France. The colleges all have more or less the same basic structure, yet every college has its own distinctive character and tradition. Lecturers and students adapt to it; changes consist of a new way of playing with old materials.

I had an entirely different experience when I lectured at a conference centre, near Namur, of the French-speaking community of Belgium. Inside this curious building, the relations between the different spaces were very unclear. The conference room had an open connection to the restaurant and the staircase which made the place very noisy. Trying to find your room was quite an expedition. You had to first go down four flights of stairs. These made you feel uncomfortable: the steps made a hollow sound and were slightly bent. Next, there were the endless corridors. You had to open badly marked doors to again finally ascend up four normal flights of stairs. The rooms had artificial numbers in the hundreds even though there were only fifty rooms.

I called this building a 'postmodern' building when I had to explain to my audience what postmodernism is or could be. A building that appears to have no plan to its visitors, a complex that was not designed to facilitate meeting and communication. At the same time it is a building you cannot stop 'talking about' when you get home. A fanciful construction, which may allow for an entirely different use of the corridors and stairways than the purpose for which they were originally built, something like the stage for a play. It is quite easy to explain what a modern building looks like. However, postmodern buildings require you to tell all kinds of stories. They reflect the complexity of our society which is difficult to navigate. We tend to get lost. It has become more difficult to share your points of view, to share common stories or be part of a tradition. Society has become less malleable. Maintaining a relationship requires constant care. The balance of power within a relationship is not permanent. Community is no longer a given. Many regard this as purely negative while others thrive on rushing from one experience to the next. In that case, the only unchanging point is my body and so the pharmaceutical industry prospers. Surveys have shown that individuality is the highest value within West-European societies. This is almost self-evident to a postmodern society. Can we still say 'we' in such a society? Can I still say 'we' and include others as a matter of course? Can others say 'we' and include me? Are 'we' still sharing something? This article aims to be little more than a survey.

Violence as the Foundation of a 'We'

I begin this survey with René Girard (1923) whom most would not normally regard as a postmodern thinker.[1] His theory can contribute to our understanding of how we ended up in our current situation and why we should definitely not return to the past. I will only discuss one aspect of his theory. Girard puts it that societies, groups, a 'we', are always based on violence. People are brought together through the use of violence. When people come together, still missing a clear structure, they see each other as a possible threat. For example, think of a school class coming together for the first time, or a meeting where nobody knows the others and the chairperson is late. As soon as the fears and uncertainties can be projected onto one person, everybody looks to him or her. A structure emerges and peace settles on all.

---

[1] R. Girard, *Deceit, Desire and the Novel,* Baltimore 1965; *Violence and the Sacred,* Baltimore 1977; *The Scapegoat,* Baltimore 1986; *Things Hidden since the Foundation of the World*. Stanford 1987; *The Victim of his People,* Stanford 1987; *Shakespeare. A Theater of Envy*, Oxford 1991.

Girard is not unique in his conviction that violence founds communities. Hannah Arendt has had the same idea.[2] They both refer to the foundation myth of Rome. Romulus kills his brother Remus and goes on to found the city. Later, Romulus himself is killed. Both Girard and Arendt refer to the bible as well. Cain builds the first city after he has murdered his brother Abel.[3] We will see how the issue of 'violence' plays an important part in the ideas about the structure of the 'we' through three postmodern philosophers, Richard Rorty, Jean-François Lyotard and Jacques Derrida, which I discuss in this article.

The original violence that unites people should be seen like a lynch mob according to Girard, although, incidentally, he does not wish to provide an historical reconstruction. People become a 'we' by collectively driving out someone from among them. By comparison with Leviticus 16 the expelled is called the 'scapegoat' and the mechanism of expulsion the 'scapegoat mechanism'. The violence of the expulsion is what binds people together. There is at first no 'we' which then proceeds to become violent, the 'we' comes about in the difference between the victim and the persecutors. Once in existence the community ascribes its origins to the victim it has itself produced. This victim becomes the mirror image of the community which did not exist before the expulsion. We can see this binding force come about before our very eyes in the violence of lynching that still takes place and, in a more veiled way, in gossip. Girard assumes that violence has been the binding force right from the beginning of human culture. It has been the foundation of the 'we' sentiment or the 'we belong together'.

The lynching that unites people was, he believes, later ritualised in sacrifice. The violence of the sacrifice – originally human sacrifice – unites people, albeit in a structured way, so that there is less chance of violent chaos. Religions are of particular social interest because they channel violence. They do this by means of the violence of sacrifice. In doing so, all religions try to unmask, lessen or even abolish violence. An important motive in the genesis of Israel is the rejection of human sacrifice where animal sacrifice takes its place. Modern Judaism does not sacrifice at all. Instead, the stories about the performance of sacrifices are only narrated.

[2] H. Arendt, *On Revolution*, Harmondsworth 1979 (1963).
[3] The murder is depicted in such stories as a killing on a first impulse or as a sacrifice. In the myth of the foundation of Rome we find traces that both Remus and Romulus were sacrificed. The senate tells the people that Romulus ascended to heaven. Kaïn calls his city Henoch, after his son Henoch. Ancient texts in the Talmud suggest that Kaïn sacrificed his son Henoch. See H. Maccoby, *The Sacred Executioner. Human Sacrifice and the Legacy of Guilt,* London 1982.

Hinduism and Buddhism no longer sacrifice animals but only incense and fruit. Islam only has one sacrifice every year and the New Testament rules out sacrifice.

The reduced visibility of violence in the sacrificial ritual and, even more so, the rejection of sacrifice altogether, mean a weakening and erosion of the binding force of the community. This 'de-sacrificialization' affects the community in its origin: its very existence is threatened. Sociologist Meerten ter Borg has pointed out, in his description of modern culture, that all religions have tried to find ways to compensate for the loss of a uniting force that emanated from sacrifice. They try to do this, for example, by putting greater emphasis on the observance of religious laws, by emphasizing the sinfulness of every person, or by reverting to the persecution of certain groups like the Jews.[4] All these means fail at an ever-increasing rate, because – partly under the influence of the gospel – the growing attention for the victim unmasks the violence that lies behind the means adopted.

Thus, Girard's theory appears to have great value for explaining what is happening in a society as that of the Netherlands. According to Girard, Christianity has promoted the loss of the binding force of sacrifice. Because of this society threatens to fall apart. The solidarity in common sacrifice disappears and all ties, in principle at least, become loose. It is no longer obvious that we always have a given 'we' like a small child always has its mother. This development invokes feelings of both fear and liberation. Fear: because we try to survive in a world without centre and try to avoid becoming a victim. Liberation: people become independent and free from the things they were bound to earlier. They are liberated from oppression and structural violence, from the violence 'from above'. In modernity the feeling of liberation held sway but in the waning of the modern age the uncertainty about how to survive increases.

Forms of 'We'

Looking at the traditional – violent – forms of human existence, we can distinguish between at least four main forms which still coexist, partially alongside each other. First, there are the *religious institutions*, by which I do not mean the organisation itself – in fact this can be absent – but the body of rites and myths, religious sacrifices and stories that legitimise these sacrifices. The second is the 'we', based on *kin*. The sovereign state,

[4] M. ter Borg, *Een uitgewaaierde eeuwigheid. Het menselijk tekort in de moderne cultuur*, Baarn 1991, 189-194.

originally connected with *kingship*, is the third form. A fourth, relatively recent form, is that of *nationalism*. Nevertheless I call this form traditional, because it expressly justifies itself by an, admittedly sometimes imaginary, tradition and lives through violence and expulsion. It is actually more of a reaction to the disappearance of the sacredness of religion, kinship and kingship than any independent form of the 'we'. We perceive these forms of 'we' as artificial creations. However, this is a modern or even postmodern point of view. Traditionally people have regarded them as 'sacred constants' and surrounded them with taboos. Modern people have robbed them of their sacredness but one can still find traces of that quality.

In this article I will assume that modernity consists in the emancipation of the individual beyond the associations already mentioned, once imposed upon people as sacrosanct. This emancipation came about in several waves. The following is a very brief, schematic description of these waves:

The sixteenth century, particularly the time of the Reformation, saw an exodus from the single religious unity. In the seventeenth century the former scientific framework was abandoned. In the eighteenth century old economic laws with their limitations of place, time, social class and above all the making of profit were left behind. In that same century, the sacred nature of the state was destroyed and exposed as fundamentally violent. This same century was the outstanding era of Enlightenment. One hundred years later the organized emancipation of the 'lower classes' started, especially of the working class, which had been formed by previous forces. Our century finally saw such thorough questioning of traditional forms of one of the most fundamental relations between people, that between men and women, that a return to the past now seems impossible. With every wave the number of people affected has increased. The weakening of the old ties was and remains accompanied by manifestations of violence, such as witch trials, religious wars, impoverishment, nationalism, terror, revolutionary violence, world wars and fundamentalism. Often, the emancipatory process means a temporary loss of freedom: for example, for a long time women were suffering from modernity rather than benefiting from it. In addition, the current force of nationalism might amaze us but the most striking aspect is probably that its violent nature is now widely recognized.

What drove people to free themselves from the old, was not just negative – the experience of oppression – but also positive, that is, the conviction that what they were doing was rational and gave them a new security. Stephen Toulmin believes the seventeenth century has been crucial in connection

---

[5] See S. Toulmin, *Cosmopolis. The Hidden Agenda of Modernity,* New York 1990.

with establishing security.⁵ René Descartes (1596-1650) and others were convinced that the only possibility to gain reliable human knowledge existed in letting go of the historical context of our questions. The ties with the audience, the readers and the researchers were abandoned and knowledge was of a general nature, timeless and universally true. Certitude was a necessary requirement, a need stemming from the historical context of that particular century, immersed in wars, a lack of safety and certainty in which one parted with the relatively static society of the Middle Ages. People wanted to wipe the slate clean. They traded a multitude of traditions for the attempt to reach one unified scientific systematisation. The old theological and philosophical disputes about doctrines no longer seemed even worthwhile.

This is how the idea that reason could be the foundation for a new 'we' came about. Especially in the eighteenth century, the Age of Enlightenment, people became convinced that human beings were essentially reasonable beings. There was widespread confidence that reason, in terms of human thinking, could unite the various unbound autonomous individuals into a 'we'. People may be closed units in themselves, but reason, information and hard evidence would bring them together. Mutual consultation, instead of orientation to the king, would unite people into a state. People believed that through dialogue, using reason as the guiding principle, any problems between individuals, groups or states could be resolved. According to Immanuel Kant (1724-1804) reason was the highest court. This confidence in reason roused a great deal of enthusiasm: *Alle Menschen werden Brüder*. For many the enthusiasm itself was an historical sign that boded well for social change. They saw it as evidence of the rationality of progress. In the nineteenth and twentieth centuries intellectuals were increasingly drawn to the cause of 'revolution', because the enthusiasm through which changes are sought prompted them to believe that history was being made, and a 'we' was being formed.

Postmodern

Calling our society 'postmodern' means that this enthusiasm and hope are vanishing. We experience that, no matter how fruitful our conversations may be, they can no longer always solve the conflicts between people. Worse still: reason, which has turned people into individuals to a much larger extent than ever before, now presumes to be generally valid and requires the submission of all. People now experience this as violence. Because of the resistance to the monopoly of reason the world becomes to an increasing extent a whole of individualities, which only partly and temporarily communicate with each other. Individuals are ships that pass each other in the night, sometimes arrive at the same port and sail away from it again. People are becoming radically autonomous. So many people, so many opinions. Multiplicity takes the place of unity.

Kant, who had proclaimed reason as the highest arbiter, already recognized that one could critically assess reason itself. It turns out that reason, for example, does not know what to do with the contrast between unity and multiplicity. One should accept both as rational. Kant has thus become one of the sources of inspiration for postmodern philosophers. They provide us with the philosophical explanation of our experience that reason is unable to create a 'we'. They want to help us appreciate the differences there are between us, and keep us from taking a generally valid, totalitarian and therefore violent point of view. We should not expect a system from them. Their philosophy is as fragmented as our society itself. They provide an analysis and try to think about the best way to act in a fragmented society. Ethical questions keep surfacing. They do not deny the existence of a 'we', but they cannot name this 'we', or can only name it negatively. By negatively I mean 'negative' in the way tradition uses the word in 'negative theology': mainly to say what God is not. Postmodern philosophers mainly tell us what is not 'we'.

Later I will briefly discuss three modern philosophers to illustrate this point. I will look into their vision of the possibility to say 'we'. The aim is not to criticize them but rather to see whether their perspective offers new openings for Christians to make a re-evaluation of their own tradition. In other words, can their ideas contribute to the discussion about coexistence in a (post)modern society?

Three Postmodern Philosophers

My first example of postmodern thinking is Richard Rorty (1931), the American philosopher.[6] He is very aware of the risk of becoming a victim in a society in which everyone has their own language, their own vocabulary, and their own network of convictions. He rejects the idea that one of those networks or the sum of those networks creates reality. The *world* is not our creation; most things in time and space have been caused without us. *Truth*, however, is only present in the sentences we string together, the words we use or, put simply, in our language. There is no truth outside lan-

---

[6] R. Rorty, *Contingency, Irony and Solidarity*, Cambridge 1989.

guage. We cannot say anything about the world and only descriptions of the world can be true or false. We shall not discover truth and falsehood by comparing our claims with the world. That is impossible, because we can only catch that world in our language. We can however compare different descriptions.[7] We have to be content in calling something the 'truth', which is in fact the outcome of conversations in which we try to convince each other without violence.[8]

Nor should we try to find solidarity – a 'we' – in something outside ourselves. There is no power that binds and unites everything. He expressly rejects the Christian notion of becoming oneself through the service of the other. There is a difference between the private world of self-realization and the world of doing justice. According to Rorty, the Christian idea that there is only one vision on life is simply not true.[9] What holds together a democratic society is little more than the fact that it gives everyone a chance to realize him or herself.[10] In our culture – the product of a certain coincidence of things – we are accustomed to giving each other that opportunity and there is no need to ask 'why'. The question 'why I would not humiliate another' is not important, but the question 'what is humiliating to another' is important. Rorty believes that the only social bond we need is the recognition that we can all be humiliated. Others can ridicule our network of beliefs or say that it is old-fashioned. In private, I am free to think and say such things. However, in society and public life I have to be aware of the great variety of ways in which others can be humiliated. What unites us with others is not that we use the same vocabulary and share the same convictions, but that we can all feel pain, and especially humiliation. We all hope that our world, our way of living and thinking, will not be destroyed.

More than philosophy, according to Rorty, literature and film sensitise us to the possibility of being humiliated. They express the pain of victims who no longer have a language themselves, because they have been robbed of it. The philosopher can only establish with a certain irony, that the sensitivity to pain is what holds us together. His work has little public meaning and is rather more suited for individual self-realization.[11] It is right to include ever more people in our solidarity, but it is wrong to believe that it exists before our recognition of this solidarity. What is at issue here is real-

---

[7] Ibid., 3-20.
[8] Ibid., 52, 67.
[9] Ibid., XIII-XVI.
[10] Ibid., 84.
[11] Ibid., 88-95.

izing that differences are unimportant in comparison to our shared sensitivity to pain and humiliation.[12] In short, we are a 'we' to the extent that we share the sensitivity to pain and humiliation.

The second postmodern philosopher is Jean-François Lyotard (1924-1998). In the book that he considers to be his most important: *The Differend* (*Le différend,* Paris 1983), he tries to unmask every 'we'. In his analysis the violence of Auschwitz is an important element. Even more than the fear of becoming a victim, he has the hope to win and survive by means of as much information as is possible.

According to Lyotard, people have different interests and different arguments that can all be equally valid. In our world many conflicts lack the possibility of securing a decision in a reasonable way. It is often not possible to do justice to one or both parties. Somebody could rightly defend the ownership of his literary work while another could correspondingly deny the possibility of such a thing ever being an object of ownership.[13] Our current political situation could be a more appealing example. A government may be right by aiming for a reduction in the budget deficit. People may be right in fighting for the maintenance of the spending power for people on relatively low incomes. This is not a conflict between a powerful government and the weak in our society. In fact, there is no litigation here, or what could be called a conflict that an impartial court of reason can decide but rather a '*différend*', a 'dispute' between two lines of argument that are both legitimate. There is no judging authority that can decide this, no supreme court that transcends everyone and everything, even an ultimate authority. Neither reason, nor the enthusiasm of revolution, for example, can give a decisive judgment.[14]

Therefore there is no 'grand narrative' anymore such as the Christian, liberal or communist narrative, in which all smaller individual stories fit. A 'great story' is a closed unit, in which the sentences are connected in a way that, both for the audience and the storyteller, a liberating whole is created and nothing unexpected can 'happen'. Such a story neutralizes all differences in favour of a struggle. For example, the 'great story' of internationalism only ever fights to conquer all national worlds. For Lyotard the world is one big theatre of different arguments and interests, which entangle people who try to achieve mastery and win. At best, one can demand that people receive the same information so that they have the same weap-

---

[12] Ibid., 192-198.
[13] J.-F. Lyotard, *The Differend. Phrases in Dispute*, Minneapolis 1988, XI.
[14] Ibid., 170; against Kant.

ons for this struggle. Politics does not just have one purpose but it has many. Politics does not aim for the good but, rather, for the lesser evil.[15] Conflicts do not come about because people are evil, but because it is impossible to do justice to everyone all the time. Peace is an agreement that temporarily and only ever solves disputes locally. One makes such a peace however within a certain space and by eschewing the *differends* on the outskirts.[16]

Among other things Lyotard analyses the declaration on the 'Rights of Man and the Citizen' of 27 August 1789. This seems to suggest a universal 'we'. According to Lyotard however it is wrong to do so. In that case, 'man' should have signed it, whereas the National Assembly, the National Assembly of France to be precise, actually signed this document. Consequently, Lyotard asks himself the question whether this is a French law or human law. Is France's war one of liberation or conquest? Should the other nations become French or human? What is more, concerning the Declaration itself: it is addressed to and informed by the presuppositions that give authority to the national laws to which we are all subject.[17] Viewed in this way, the Declaration actually amounts to a call for constant civil war. The statement 'we the people of France' assumes that the one issuing the law and the one subject to the law are the same and form a united 'we'. In other words, we proclaim a norm that says that it is our duty to do this or that. There is no real 'we' present, however. The people issuing the law and those subject to it are not in the same place.

This difference between the one issuing the law and, the one subject to it, according to Lyotard, becomes very important when the subject is told to die as a result of the law. In other words, it is *not* the order to die that creates the 'we'. Traditionally there has always been such a thing as a 'beautiful death'. The victim then would be able to identify with the lawgiver who gives the orders to die. This means that the victim's name is, in a sense, part of the collective. The victim escapes death because he lives on, maybe not in his own name, but at least as a part of the collective. In ancient Athens the dead had the right to be called Athenians. The 'we' of ancient Athens consisted of the living that spoke about the dead heroes, and the dead themselves. A good death is a prerogative that was derived from a good birth.[18]

According to Lyotard Auschwitz was the prohibition for a beautiful death. The authority of the SS is founded on a 'we' that excludes the Jew,

[15] Ibid., 138-141.
[16] Ibid., 151.
[17] Ibid., 145-147.
[18] Ibid., 97-100; 104-110.

the deportee. The deportees cannot give their life, because they do not have the right to life. Their death is legal, because their life is not. A court is not needed at Auschwitz. The aim is not just to kill the individual, but also the Jewish collective, so that no name remains to immortalize the name of the deportee. Witnesses and evidence are destroyed together with the victims. The one issuing the order is not subject to this order to die. The deportees cannot take their place and identify with their executor. In Auschwitz every 'we' is an illusion. The SS and the deportees live in two entirely different worlds. Auschwitz yielded nothing, certainly no 'we', not even after Auschwitz.[19]

For Lyotard Auschwitz is the impossibility to think in terms of totals or to form any kind of 'we'. At the same time, according to Lyotard, obliging other people to do something can never lead to a universal community. This is also true of the commandment to love each other.[20] Such a commandment presupposes the existence of 'one' world. However, there are always many worlds. In our society people often suggest that the 'great narrative' of the free market is creating one world. Critics of the modern economy are complaining that it surpasses all traditional forms and dominates and colonises them. Lyotard points out that the economy does not pose the ethical question, rather, the economy can never have a universal meaning as such, nor can it ever form a true 'we'.[21]

According to Lyotard we can only think about the impossibility of forming a 'we'. The 'we' will always be a 'we' of people that admittedly have unsolvable disputes with each other and therefore actually do not form a 'we'. Only in this way, can there still be something like a 'we'. This 'we' consists of a 'me' that is writing this and a 'you' that is reading it.[22] In doing so the 'me' is constantly trying to unmask the violent totality of a 'we' and foster the sensitivity to the differences.

By mentioning the relation between writer and reader, we can 'link onto' – a word that Lyotard likes to use – Jacques Derrida (1930-2004). Even more clearly than Lyotard, Derrida writes in the margins of what others have published.[23] He analyses their texts with great sagacity. He is constantly trying to expose the hidden presuppositions to the text. He believes that what is forgotten has either not been thought of or left out of a text but di-

---

[19] Ibid., 100-106.
[20] Ibid., 159-161.
[21] Ibid., 178-179.
[22] Ibid., 103.
[23] This causes problems when one tries to interpret Derrida. See G. Bennington and J. Derrida, *Jacques Derrida*, Chicago 1993.

rects the text and gives it its content. He does not take a position, and even when he does, he is not prepared to defend it unconditionally. I think Derrida is more thorough than Rorty and Lyotard. In his works, violence is very much a recurring theme. Without explicitly referring to a 'we' to whom the individual has to conform, Derrida rejects the idea that anything substantial is given. By doing so, he ends any possibility to think in terms of an unchanging 'being'. This *ipso facto* proposes a given 'we'.

A good example of his thought is his wonderful study of Plato's Pharmacy.[24] To the Greek philosopher Plato (427-347 BC), our world is a copy of the everlasting and unchanging 'being', of the one, the true, the good. The possibility for us, a multitude of people, to form a 'we' is based on the existence of this 'world of the ideas'. People keep a memory of this world in their minds. It is remarkable in his dialogue *Phaedrus* as well as in other texts that Plato turns against writing, even though he writes himself and has other people writing down his words. He defends his writing as a kind of pastime. Derrida shows that according to Plato a written text has a function only because of the absence of the actual, the true, and being itself. A spoken argument lives, behaves, like a person and, like any living being, has a father, namely the good, being, the true, which is identical to itself and present for itself. This spoken argument comes straight from 'memory', which is its messenger. A written text, on the other hand, comes from someone who is a messenger himself. Such a text disconnects truth from its origin. It expresses the longing for the status of an orphan which in Plato's works is synonymous to that of the accused, for a written text is the result of what he sees as the worst form of violence: patricide. The written text puts itself in the place of the father and pushes him away, like the moon replaces the sun, in its absence. Plato wrote this after the death of Socrates, whom he regards as the firstborn son, because in his words he represented the father, the world of the ideas.

In the myth of the birth of writing, which Plato relates in the *Phaedrus*, writing is recommended as a drug, a medicine, a *pharmakon*, for remembering things. In Greek, and in the works of Plato, the word *pharmakon* has many meanings: sperm, ink, paint, perfume, gift, and poison. Socrates was executed with poison. It is something that penetrates everything such as water. Derrida adds that *pharmakon* also means 'scapegoat' though he attaches no special meaning to this.[25] Plato argues that writing is a dangerous medicine. It is both a gift and a poison. It is damaging and unhealthy be-

---

[24] J. Derrida, *Dissemination,* London 1981, 61-171.
[25] See for a discussion on the similarities and differences between Girard and Derrida: A. J. McKenna, *Violence and Difference. Girard, Derrida, and Deconstruction*, Chicago 1982.

cause it goes against natural life. It is good for that memory which only has to repeat something, but it is bad for the living 'memory' that knows the world of eternal ideas, that is, for 'being'. According to Plato writing harms the 'memory'. Derrida thinks he dreams of an immediate knowing without writing and even without words or signs, in other words, without mediation.

Derrida however shows that Plato cannot do without this *pharmakon*. When he speaks of the true, he has to use the metaphor of writing: the truth is, in fact, written in the soul. Writing in the soul is loftier than writing on paper. Writing on paper is the prodigal and orphaned son, is the trace that causes the true to be lost. Again, in his description of the creation of the world, Plato cannot avoid the metaphor of writing: the fatherly forms are written within a motherly matrix, which in itself has no form or presence at all. When he speaks about the oneness and multitude, he can only repeat the 'murder of the father' of philosophy, Parmenides (c 540-475 BC), the philosopher of oneness, by pointing to different letters that together form a whole. Every time Plato has to indicate a difference he feels compelled to use the metaphor of writing. He cannot speak about 'being' without the mediation of signs, that is, without referring to differences.

According to Derrida Plato shows that, despite himself, the 'true' can only manifest itself to us, if the 'true' and the 'being-identical-to-itself' are absent. What is 'not-being', 'not-truth' and 'not-presence' – a written text – 'is', according to Derrida, truth and presence. What is identical to itself is only there because of its possibility to be replaced and repeated. It is there thanks to the *pharmakon* of writing. Derrida concludes that there is no presence, no being given, no truth or goodness. The reality to which signs are supposed to refer is missing. The origin of everything starts with the difference; something that he calls 'différance', and which only differs from 'différence' in the way it is written. Somewhere else, he writes: the 'différance'

> derives from no category of being, whether present or absent. And yet those aspects of 'différance' which are thereby delineated, are not theological, not even in the order of the most negative of negative theologies, which are always concerned with disengaging a super-essentiality beyond the finite categories of essence and existence, that is, of presence, and always hastening to recall that God is refused the predicate of existence, only in order to acknowledge his superior, inconceivable, and ineffable mode of being. Such a development is not in question here. (…) There is nowhere to begin to trace the sheaf or the graphics of 'différance'. For what is put into question is precisely the quest for a rightful beginning, an absolute point of departure, a principal responsibility. (…) No transcendent truth present outside the field of writing can govern theologically the totality of the field.[26]

Derrida's line of reasoning signals the emancipation of the individual from eternal and unchanging truths. However, the absence of a given presence of being does not mean we are completely free. We have been given texts. However, according to Derrida, no text, not even his own, has an absolute, established meaning. After all, that would imply a presence of the truth, which controls a world of meanings, like a god. When reading texts, every reader does so in his or her way. Every reading is an interpretation, every interpretation changes something in the meaning and to some extent violates the text. Writer and reader constantly owe something to each other. The reader has the writer to thank for his text. But the writer is indebted to the reader, for he still exists simply because he is read even though he may not be present or may even be dead. The text wants to be read. The writer's autograph requires the reader's autograph. However, the text itself is given to us. Language is imposed upon us like a law. It is forced upon us. It is a gift that we have to accept before we can say anything else. We have no choice. It is a necessity, and this necessity is the cause of violence. Like any other gift, the gift of language poisons us.

Derrida believes people cannot avoid reacting to or speaking about the other. Language is necessary and as such a form of violence. Yet, speaking to someone and about someone is still better than ignoring them. Conversation is a war against that silence, a war against nihilism, a war against that war. Whenever there is peace, it is determined and protected by the violence of the 'word'. The conversation is violent, but it is the minimum possible form of violence. Derrida rejects the idea of absolute non-violence – after all, the absolute does not exist. He argues for an 'economy of violence' – economy in the sense of being 'economical'.[27] History is the time of violence. However, we can try to find less violence or the least violence. The relations we are faced with are, at the very least, also characterised by violence.

A Theological Perspective

Can the Christian tradition learn anything from and contribute anything to the discussion about the question whether we can still say 'we' in our postmodern society? I can only give an initial reaction here. Christians have continually called for the formation of a 'we'. For theology and church practice this meant that individuals should join a 'we' that already existed

---

[26] J. Derrida, *Margins of Philosophy*, Chicago 1972, 6-7.
[27] Idem, Violence and Metaphysics. An Essay on the Thought of Emmanuel Levinas, in: *Writing and Difference*, London 1978, 79-153; here 125-129.

as an unchanging reality: the dogmatic argument formulated for eternity; the indisputable ethical law, the sacrosanct church, an unchanging God as the creator of all being.

Do its texts offer any other ways of forming a 'we'? I have to fall back on one of the primary texts of the Christian story: the story of the Good Samaritan in Luke 10:30-35, ignoring the general context of the story. I believe this story takes violence seriously, mentions an alternative possibility of forming a 'we' and at the same time provides an opening for the criticism of the postmodern philosophers that I have mentioned in this article. The tale runs as follows:

> A man was on his way from Jerusalem down to Jericho when he fell in with robbers, who stripped him, beat him, and went off leaving him half dead. It so happened that a priest was going down by the same road; but when he saw him, he went past on the other side. So too a Levite came to the place, and when he saw him went past on the other side. But a Samaritan who was making the journey came upon him, and when he saw him, was moved to pity. He went up and bandaged his wounds, bathing them with oil and wine. Then he lifted him on to his own beast, brought him to an inn, and looked after him there. Next day he produced two silver pieces and gave them to the innkeeper, and said, "Look after him; and if you spend any more, I will repay you on my way back."

This story features different notions of 'we'. The robbers are clearly a 'we'. They form a tightly knit 'we' thanks to their violence towards their victim. The story tells us nothing about their individuality. They are one in their violence against a person who travels on the road between Jerusalem and Jericho. The priest and the Levite also form a 'we'. Their 'we' is weaker: they do not know of each other's existence in this story. Hierarchically, the priest is superior to the Levite: though they do relate to the victim in an identical way. They both went past on the other side. Furthermore, they both have a connection to the temple in which sacrifices are made every day. The Samaritan and the victim will form a 'we'; this also happens between the Samaritan and the innkeeper and, because of that, between the innkeeper and the victim. In every 'we' the victim is the common binding element.

The characters in the story differ from each other. They each have their own argument and these arguments are mostly controversial. The robbers and the victim have a 'dispute'. No authority can solve this dispute and create a mutual accommodation. The victim survives the attack, but if he had died, he would not have had a 'beautiful death'. In their sermons, clergymen have often depicted the priest and the Levite as heartless. However, they have their own arguments. According to Jewish law, anyone touching the body of a dead person is unclean for seven days; on the third day after incurring the uncleanness, an extensive ritual is necessary to lift the uncleanness (Num. 19:1-22). Clean and unclean help to determine who is and who is not part of the Jewish community. The priest and the Levite are very much the guardians of these boundaries. They have a heart for a community that exists through its relation to the sacrifices in the temple. This is what makes them pass on the other side. The fact that the victim is 'half dead' symbolises the uncertainty that keeps recurring when a 'we' is demarcated. The Samaritan and the victim also have a different discourse. The story suggests that the victim is a Jew. Jews and Samaritans both claimed Moses but they did not accept each other's religious claims. Here, again, there is no authority to solve this dispute. The Samaritan, who is travelling and the innkeeper, who earns a living from travellers, have different interests and different arguments. There is no real 'we' between them. The traveller can link onto the argument of the innkeeper and give him some money, but a traveller without money does not exist as such for the innkeeper.

Violence gets the story going. The passers-by and the innkeeper are not personally confronted with the violence, but with the trace of violence in the person of the victim. The story has a *pharmakon* that directs it, but this is not hidden and does not lie outside the story. The *pharmakon* is as large as life: the victim lying on the road. In this story, it is not a sign without reference to a (non-existent) presence; the victim is no sign of language, but refers to himself. He has been robbed, and lies there like an orphan, a persecuted one, half dead and therefore almost entirely absent, yet so present. His body is like a poison that one should avoid, but it turns out that it can also be a gift, so that life continues.

The three passers-by see the victim. It is certain that fear and sensitivity to pain connects them to the victim. However, this solidarity remains highly abstract. Only the third passer-by acts. He no doubt knows the commandment that states that one must also help an enemy in need (Ex. 23:4-5), but this story does not refer to that case. The Samaritan does not act in accordance with a principle or from the idea of love. He is affected in his own body ('in his guts') – the words 'moved to pity' in the translation are already a further interpretation. It is not enthusiasm – a form of fascination – that drives him to act, nor is it a reasoned argument, nor the idea that he can fulfil himself this way. His actions are not those of a potential victim, because his actions make him increasingly vulnerable to potential robbers. This bodily affectedness is the real *pharmakon* of the story. Here, it only has the positive meaning of a healing gift and it is not hidden.

This affectedness drives the Samaritan to act pharmaceutically, nursing the wounds, transporting him to the inn and making sure he is looked after. It happens, but as such, this cannot be explained, cannot be imagined, named or expected.

The Samaritan and the innkeeper form a 'we' to the extent that the first is a paying traveller and the latter is an innkeeper paid by him. This is an economic 'we'. In economics victims only have a value if they bring in money. To the innkeeper, the victim is a source of income. The 'we' between the innkeeper and the victim is also economic by nature. Both know this; the innkeeper can safely give the Samaritan credit. The Samaritan gives the victim his economic value. The victim as victim has no value. He has been stripped, is half dead, unable to produce.

The 'we' between the Samaritan and the innkeeper and that between the innkeeper and the victim come about because of the 'we' between the Samaritan and the victim. The 'we' of the Samaritan and the victim is the 'we' that drives the story. Is there a 'we' at all? For modern people, there can only be a 'we' when two or more persons face each other as equals. Our story implies a certain dependency on the other and, therefore, a difference. The victim cannot contribute anything as such, and does not even have to be aware of what is happening. The Samaritan is his aid. As with the robbers, a 'we' is formed based on the difference between the victim and the other(s). However, this 'we' comes about in an alternative way. It is not the violation of the body of the other, but being affected bodily, the care for and service to the body of the stranger, that founds the community and drives economic actions. While the violence nullifies the body and thus denies the difference again so that new violence is necessary to maintain the 'we', care saves the body of the other and respects the difference. This care precedes language, which, if not in its origin, at least in its actual application is interwoven with violence. Therefore, it cannot be fully explained and given a name by language. It cannot be organised; it will forever be a small wonder when it takes place. At best, one can create conditions that make the miracle more likely to happen.

In the care for the victim, the Samaritan emancipates himself from his own religion, the 'we' he was raised in, the tradition of hate against the Jews. Unlike the old, the new 'we' is not a permanent and unchanging order; nothing indicates that the Samaritan and the (recovered) victim will stay chained to each other. The Samaritan's actions are unexpected and unique. What is true, however, is that wherever people tell this story, it creates an alternative for a different 'we'. The world, in which we normally have to accept an 'economy' of violence, becomes a different place for a short while.

This story has its special context but without any abstract arguments. That is why it can never be repeated literally; as soon as anyone tries, it loses its meaning. It is a testimony to the existence of alternatives; it invites the telling of comparable stories, and above all, unexpected 'pharmaceutical' actions. One cannot make these actions compulsory as with a law. Traditionally, Christian language and reflection denote the actions of the Samaritan as a commandment. What really happens, however, is not the fulfilment of a commandment, but grace, an unexpected gift, another small miracle. This is what the current context of the story tells us.

In the context of the gospel story a lawyer is looking for a general commandment: define for me the neighbour I have to love. The 'neighbour' is a technical term for the one who forms a 'we' together with you (Lev. 19:17-18). The lawyer asks for the limits of the 'we'. This appears to be the wrong question. The answer is: be like the Samaritan, allow the miracle to enter your life and discover who your neighbour is. There is no conclusive 'we', no identity that is fixed beforehand. Even when 'love', 'service' or 'mercy' are included in the language of tradition, this language does not guarantee that they actually take place; mercy is always unexpected. The 'we' is forever created anew and cannot be fixed.

Postmodern thought challenges Christians to free themselves from the compulsion to conform to a tradition and identity that Christians often present as unchanging. It explains the questions many Christians have about the way in which they have so far tried to form a community. Over against the postmodern panic – often represented as an ironic game – the Christian stories tell of an unexpected breakthrough of an alternative 'we'. This alternative does not exist as a mirror image of an eternal, unchanging God, but is instead rooted in being affected bodily by a victim. This 'being moved' can be experienced as a gift of transcendence, from a God who is encountered in and through a speechless victim on the road.

Alienation as Identity

Believing in Cultivated Vulnerability

Erik Borgman

Introduction

During the first centuries of Christianity, though it may not have been such a turbulent time as ours, people's trust in the infinite power of the 'heavenly court' was apparently stronger. In those years of early Christianity the very image of faith and redemption, and its meaning for the human soul, was expressed by the scene of the three men in the baptism of the fiery furnace from the third chapter of the book of Daniel. Here it narrates the story of how they refused to adore the statue King Nebuchadnezar erected to the sacredness of his power and how he had them cast into the fiery furnace as a punishment. In the Greek version of this story they continue to praise God amidst the flames and thereby call up an angel who re-creates a climate in the oven 'as though a whistling breeze were blowing through it' (Dan. 3:24ff).[1] The story was interpreted as a reference to heaven, the place where, far from any appearances, human integrity – the 'soul' – is kept.[2]

However, after the horrors of the twentieth century heaven has been shattered. This is what the Dutch writer and sculptor Jan Wolkers wanted to illustrate when he designed a monument to the ultimate symbol of these horrors, consisting of large fragments from a mirror to commemorate the massive systematic killing in Auschwitz. It reflects a broken heaven and expresses the experience that, unlike the first generations of Christians, we will never again have the same certainty about our identity. Our history has definitively shown us that faith and loyalty alone cannot redeem us. For there are moments when the dew-laden breeze should blow but does not. With the loss of the heavenly image as the place where everything is held together in spite of all external crises, the image of the world and of ourselves is also shattered. As if to emphasize this, one of the people involved in the construction of the Auschwitz monument broke the fragments of the mirror with

---

[1] Part of the book of Daniel has been handed down in Hebrew, part only in Greek. Protestants do not regard the latter as canonical, but Catholics do, following the example of the early church. This means it is seen as an integral part of the bible as 'holy scripture'.

[2] J.J.M. Timmers, *Christelijke symboliek en iconografie*, Haarlem ³1978, 188-189.

a sledgehammer into even smaller pieces.

Apparently, we cannot just pick up the pieces and carry on. We cannot live with mere brokenness. However, just as Wolkers' monument does not express the experience of brokenness passively, but rather stylises it, it appears to me to be the task of faith and theology 'after Auschwitz' to shape and construct an identity that expresses that brokenness in a way that makes it bearable. In this chapter, I would like to show that both the Judaic and the Christian traditions offer potential starting points for such an identity.

Identity as a Flexible Foundation

We can only speak of identity, as a more or less consistent image of the self in the midst of many historical changes and developments, when people cease to naturally coincide with the defined roles they have in society. In a perfectly stable and closed society – if such an entity ever existed – there is no room for personal identity and no pressure to develop one. This implies that identity is never entirely self-evident. Identity is also always a matter of choice and therefore presupposes, to a certain extent, freedom. There is probably no form of society that completely lacks this freedom. Moreover, in the West, classical philosophy and the Jewish and Christian traditions have always contributed substantially to an awareness of the value of the individual versus tradition and social relations. Nevertheless, the idea of a personal identity, as we now know it, has only developed since the beginning of the modern age.

With the emergence of the modern age increasing numbers of people experience that they are not simply part of the larger scheme of things, but that they can also change that larger scheme, the world and culture they are confronted with.[3] They are no longer merely subject to social relations but they are also able to act in such a way that can either maintain or change these relations. Modern thinking generally regards human beings as 'subjects' of action; as free, rational sources of thoughts and acts that they choose for themselves. The word 'subject' also means 'somebody who is subject to', and therefore, this constitutes a hidden clue to the fact that freedom is realized in bondage. It discovers its form in the limited space a society allots to people, and in the process it uses the cultural tradition, made

---

[3] See A. Giddens, *Modernity and Self-Identity. Self and Society in the Late Modern Age*, Cambridge 1991.

available within that civilization.[4] In contrast with the prevailing emphasis on autonomy, characteristic of modern philosophy, postmodern philosophers focus on the importance of the coincidental and the given, the uncontrollable. Based on this, 'identity' can be seen as the place where the 'given' and the 'shaping' converge. Biological data, cultural traditions, social structures and role patterns come about because someone adopts them as qualities and takes them as starting points for his or her actions and thoughts. In a way, the world becomes your world, even if it is the world in which you do not feel at home; your body becomes your body, even though you are unhappy with that body; and life becomes your life, even though you would prefer or try very hard to live it differently. On the basis of this appropriation, people can act within the boundaries of the relative freedom given to them.

Identity in this sense is probably a necessary condition for every human action. However, its importance increases as the power of the structures that give people their meaningful place in society decreases. The focus of today's media on 'human interest' and personal feelings, the significance people attach to 'lifestyle' and to attributes that symbolize a personal choice within the offer of contemporary culture, clearly shows how central the identity of a person is to contemporary society. At the same time, the fact that 'lifestyle' is subject to fashion, also shows that current, postmodern identity is not established once and for all. The synthesis that transforms the given to a starting point for acting, is under constant pressure, because the social given and the things considered to be culturally important are subject to fundamental change. It is part of a postmodern situation and a postmodern idea of life that identity is something changeable and flexible.

Religious Identity: Strong or Weak?

Apparently, it is neither society nor a specific subculture within it that functions as the basis for modern individuals, but the 'forever-new' creation of their personal identity. This is clearly demonstrated in our current, postmodern situation. Yet in the days when the social landscape was dominated by large social movements and their subcultures from the last decades of the 19th century till the 1960's, the identity of people was also a central idea. In those days social democrat and communist, Protestant and Catholic politics were certainly not exclusively aimed at controlling and organizing society.

---

[4] See G. Therborn, *The Ideology of Power and the Power of Ideology*, London 1980, 16-17.

Of equal importance were the battle for the hearts and souls of people, including attempts to awaken in them a sense of being socialist or protestant, communist or catholic.

Since the last quarter of the 19th century, Catholicism – to which I will limit myself in this chapter – had become less and less an environment into which people were naturally born and had to find their place. Being a Catholic had increasingly become a well-defined identity, a whole-heartedly accepted way of dealing with the problems of modern life.[5] For example, it implied following the choices that the leaders of the movement made in their vision on society. These were detailed in official Catholic social doctrines following the papal encyclical *Rerum Novarum*, published in 1891. According to this doctrine, social unrest and rising international tensions were the result of a modern desire for freedom and the fact that people increasingly turned away from the authority of the church. Being a Catholic meant a commitment to the Catholic counter-society and membership in as many Catholic social organizations as possible. It also meant leading a life immersed in numerous concrete rituals, including Sunday – or preferably daily – churchgoing and Holy Communion, frequent prayer and other observances. All these ways of behaving were meant to demonstrate visibly and palpably that it made sense to understand your station in life and shape it with the help of Catholic tradition. It offered a concrete possibility to feel safe and sheltered in an otherwise turbulent and sometimes threatening world. Church authorities wanted to invite people to shape themselves as 'Catholic'.

At least in the Netherlands Catholicism, as a cohesive social movement, disintegrated in the 1960's and 70's. For many reasons the militant anti-modern stance of the Church quickly lost its effectiveness and credibility after the Second World War. It had already come under severe pressure in some places during the period between the wars. At the Second Vatican Council (1962-1965), the Catholic Church emphatically opened itself to modern developments and, instead of its distance to the changing and confusing world, it expressed its solidarity with it from that moment on. Given this historical background, it was quite surprising that an official church document should read:

---

[5] This vision, which is only explained briefly here, is generally based on the way in which historians at the Catholic University of Nijmegen studied Catholicism as a social movement in the line of M. G. Spiertz and J.H. Roes.

The joys and hopes, the grief and anguish of the people of our time, especially of those who are poor or afflicted, are the joys and hopes, the grief and anguish of the followers of Christ as well. (...) That is why they cherish a feeling of deep solidarity with the human race and its history.[6]

The question about which Catholic – Christian, religious – identity matches this attitude to the world and how this could find its shape has not really been answered yet. However, many suggestions can be found in the lives of Catholics and in the developments that their organisations went through.[7]

For a minority of Catholics, the lack of clarity this change caused was a reason for distancing themselves from the conciliar openness to the modern age. They generally regarded the social developments of the years after 1965 as increased chaos and relativisation of all values, but especially religious values. They believe that it was the church's duty in this situation to offer people a 'safe-haven from modernity'. However, this minority is very influential. Joseph Ratzinger, the current Pope Benedict XVI and Prefect of the Roman Congregation for the Doctrine of the Faith during the pontificate of Karol Wojtyla, John Paul II, is part of this group.[8] As distinct from their penchant for a strong identity that creates a distinct profile for itself against the world, I would prefer to maintain that only a weak, vulnerable identity will do justice to the situation we currently live in, at least for those who, in agreement with the Second Vatican Council, set store by our solidarity with those who 'are poor or afflicted'. However, in this case, a weak identity is not necessarily an indistinct one.

---

[6] Pastoral Constitution on the Church in the Modern World *Gaudium et Spes*, no. 1.

[7] See E. Borgman, B. van Dijk, Th. Salemink (eds), *De vernieuwingen in katholiek Nederland. Van Vaticanum II tot Acht Mei Beweging*, Amersfoort 1988; E. Borgman, B. van Dijk, Th. Salemink (eds), *Katholieken in de moderne tijd. Een onderzoek door de Acht Mei Beweging*, Zoetermeer 1995; E. Borgman, De kerk als schijnbaar fundament. Over het zwijgen van de theologie, en het doorbreken daarvan, in: *Tijdschrift voor Theologie* 35 (1995) 358-372.

[8] See for K. Wojtyla: H. Häring, Kerk, wat zeg je van jezelf? De theologie van Johannes Paulus II, in: *Tijdschrift voor Theologie* 25 (1985) 229-249; voor Ratzinger: id., Eine katholische Theologie? J. Ratzinger, das Trauma von Hans im Glück, in: N. Greinacher, H. Küng (eds), *Katholische Kirche wohin?*, München 1986, 241-258; L. Boeve, Kerk, theologie en heilswaarheid. De klare taal van Joseph Ratzinger, in: *Tijdschrift voor Theologie* 33 (1993) 139-164. The intellectual mouthpiece of this movement is the international Catholic magazine *Communio*.

Alienated Identity

One could seriously ask oneself whether the bishops, who eventually approved the documents of the Second Vatican Council, really knew what they were doing. Did they realise what the actual consequences were of trying to take seriously the history of the twentieth century, with the excessive suffering that people have inflicted upon each other and have been subjected to?

These events have cast grave doubts on the social fabric, not least on religious and theological thought itself. The Jewish theologian Irving Greenberg reflects that, 'after the horrors of Auschwitz, no statement can be made, theologically or otherwise, unless it remains credible in the presence of children being burned.' He argues for a theological silence, because even simple speaking about God's presence and involvement has lost its credibility after the great horror.[9] And for the Jewish theologian André Neher, Auschwitz means 'the exile of the word.'[10] The postmodern philosopher Jean-François Lyotard is even more emphatic. According to him, after Auschwitz even language itself has lost its coherency, and with it its meaning, because Auschwitz definitively ended any possibility to say 'we'. Two groups have permanently become each other's opposites, those that killed and those that were killed, and their worlds were fundamentally different. That is why we cannot say anything meaningful about Auschwitz – and therefore about the whole violent history of the twentieth century, of which Auschwitz is the unspeakable condensation. Saying something meaningful about Auschwitz would mean that we would have to be the SS-officer and the deportee alternately.[11]

Yet Lyotard, as do Greenberg and Neher, does speak after Auschwitz. He even speaks *about* Auschwitz and the relation of Auschwitz to our culture. According to him, after Auschwitz, our culture permanently split between that of the perpetrators and that of the victims, and thus every self-evident identity has been broken. However, Lyotard – in my view – can only say this because he feels hurt by Auschwitz, even though he was not one of the deportees and at the same time knows he is part of the same culture that made Auschwitz possible, even though he was not an SS-officer. Neither a

---

[9] I. Greenberg, Cloud of Smoke, Pillar of Fire. Judaism, Christianity, and Modernity after the Holocaust, in: E. Fleischner (ed.), *Auschwitz. Beginning of a New Era?*, New York 1977, 7-55, here 23.

[10] Ibid. 41; A. Neher, *L'exil de la parole. Du silence biblique au silence d'Auschwitz*, Paris 1970.

[11] J.-F. Lyotard, *Le Différend*, Paris 1983, 152; According to Lyotard, his whole postmodern philosophy is an attempt to answer the question of how it is possible to speak after Auschwitz.

victim, nor a perpetrator himself, he is still connected to both in different ways and establishes his identity from this position: the identity of someone who, after Auschwitz, will forever be alien to any unequivocal determination of identity, and will have to live with this alienation.

In line with this, the American Lutheran theologian Darrell Fasching shows in his book, *Narrative Theology After Auschwitz: From Alienation to Ethics*, to what extent Christians have become alien within their own tradition after Auschwitz, and to what extent that alienation is part of a credible Christian identity.[12] He argues that early in Christianity it came to regard itself as the successor and heir to Judaism. According to Fasching, this already e-merged after the destruction of the temple in the year 70 AD, and traces of this line of thought can be found in significant sections of the New Testament itself. Auschwitz has shown just how devastating it is when Christians think that, now that the Jews have forfeited their chance in God's covenant, they are the new people of God, implying that the covenant with the Jews has lost its validity. Theologising about the replacement of Judaism by Christianity, the vilification of existing Judaism and the Jews, are directly connected to the destruction of the Jewish people.[13] Christians and their tradition are not just accessory to Auschwitz and the violence, oppression and death it symbolizes, but they are also stricken by it. The liberation and human dignity that to both Christians and Jews is 'of God' have been violated with inconceivable radicality at Auschwitz.

Accordingly, for Fasching, Christian tradition has both helped make Auschwitz possible and has been tarnished by it. This is why he thinks a Christian identity after Auschwitz can only be that of an alien within the tradition. Christian identity has become an alienated, broken identity, and he believes it should remain that way. This aspect in particular strikes me as being the main concern of Fasching's ideas. He is not interested in undoing the alienation vis-à-vis the Christian tradition as soon as possible by identifying the elements that keep us from a complete endorsement of that identity and

---

[12] D.J. Fasching, *Theology after Auschwitz. From Alienation to Ethics*, Minneanapolis 1992. For my views on this book, see E. Borgman, Van identiteit naar vervrecmding. De betekenis van Darrell J. Faschings '*Vreemdeling na Auschwitz*', in: A. van Harskamp (ed.), *Geloof en vertrouwen na Auschwitz*, Zoetermeer 1995, 60-74.

[13] See H. Jansen, *Christelijke theologie na Auschwitz. I: Theologische en kerkelijke wortels van het antisemitisme*, 's-Gravenhage 1981; H. Schreckenberg, *Die christlichen Adversus-Judaeos-Texte und ihr literarisches und historisches Umfeld (1.-11. Jh.)*, Frankfurt am Main ²1990; id., *Die christlichen Adversus-Judaeos-Texte (11.-13. Jh.)*, Frankfurt am Main 1988; idem, *Die christlichen Adversus-Judaeos-Texte und ihr literarisches und historisches Umfeld (13.-20.Jh.)*, Frankfurt am Main 1994.

subsequently eradicating them. The point at issue, for Fasching, is not having an anti-Jewish Christian identity replaced by a Christian identity that consciously associates itself with elements of Judaism. It is having a strong, undisputed identity that is itself problematic. The strong and constant faith that has traditionally been regarded as a virtue in Christianity is directly related to the way of thinking that enabled the executors of the mass destruction of the Jews to do their work. They sacrificed themselves and their own ability to judge and completely devoted themselves to the 'cause' that they thought served the salvation of humanity and which they believed they should remain with: the total destruction of the Jewish people. They took this to such extremes that they did not even see the concrete pain and misery of people and were able to be executioner and dedicated family man at the same time.

'Nothing ever deserves our absolute, unquestioning loyalty, not even our God, because this will always lead to the possibility of SS-loyalty', states Fasching, in agreement with Irving Greenberg.[14] Instead, it is the people who are unsure about who they are, where to go and what to say who are, according to Fasching, credible, because these people have been cast out of their natural context and are trying to live with this fact: they turn alienation itself into the basis for their identity.

A Frank Indictment

Thinking about the way in which such an identity could find its concrete form, Fasching tries to find a connection to the Jewish tradition of 'choetzpah', of frankness and courage. He believes this tradition offers an alternative to the emphasis on obedience to God that also plays an important part in Judaism. Whereas the latter has become massively dominant in Christianity, Judaism also has 'a different expression of the covenant [with God]. In this idea of the covenant, it is as if God and the Jewish people have grown up together and therefore treat each other with the familiarity of old friends or lovers'.[15]

The covenant is regarded as a mutual contract: the Jewish people commit themselves to living in accordance with God's commandments, and God

---

[14] D.J. Fasching, o.c., 52. See I. Greenberg, Cloud of Smoke, Pillar of Fire, 38.
[15] D.J. Fasching, o.c., 45; D.J. Fasching is quoting A. Laytner, *Arguing with God. A Jewish Tradition*, Northvale 1990, xvi-xvii.

commits to being with His people, leading them and protecting them. Whenever one or both parties fails to keep their end of the deal, there is room for discussion, indictment and reproach. Not just from God to the people, but also from the people to God. The latter is a case of 'choetzpah', of 'frankness towards heaven'. This choetzpah cannot just be found in the texts passed down from the Old Testament prophets and old Jewish sages, but also in the indictment of the God who failed to support the people in the death camps, as Elie Wiesel articulates this in his writings.[16] 'The ethics of choetzpah appeals to God against God in the name of God's creation', surmises Fasching; he sees Abraham in his debate with God about the destruction of Sodom (Gen. 22), Jacob in his struggle with the stranger at the river Jabbok (Gen. 32:22-32) and especially Job in his indictment against, and his struggle with God, as embodiments of this frankness towards heaven.

Jesus too is rooted in this tradition. Fasching considers Jesus as somebody who challenges all authority in the tradition of choetzpah and in the name of human dignity, even where this authority calls upon God. He believes, quite classically, that Christian identity consists in the imitation of Christ; the Christian faith is, in his view, faithful to the things Jesus incorporated and which are divine in their origins, following the Christian tradition. Fasching formulates this as 'surrender to the Logos that questions every authority in the name of human dignity'. He combines this with the – very classical – idea that 'Jesus ... is "not yet" messiah.' And he proposes that Christians join the Jewish conviction that, as long as the messianic age of peace and justice has not started, the messiah has apparently not arrived yet. He believes the New Testament expectation of the second coming of Christ as the messiah means that the first generations of Christians also believed that Jesus still had to become the messiah. 'Like the Jews, the Christians are still waiting for the messiah to come'. Fasching interprets the provisional awarding of the title 'messiah' and 'Christ' to Jesus as

> an eschatological deed of faith and hope that one day a new era will begin, which has been announced by Jesus, when suffering, injustice and death can no longer threaten human dignity.

Accordingly, it is essentially about the Christian being drawn into the messianic hope that Jews and Christians restore the true 'role of Israel/Jacob ...

---

[16] D.J. Fasching, *o.c.*, 47-53. In his idea of choetzpah, D.J. Fasching relies strongly on B. Lane, Hutzpa K'lapei Shamaya. A Christian Response to the Jewish Tradition of Arguing with God, in: *Journal of Ecumenical Studies* 23 (1986) 567-586.

who wrestled with God and with people for the sake of God and humanity' and have the courage to frankly and impatiently ask: God, how much longer![17]

After Auschwitz, this constitutes a direction, not just to break from a number of aspects from the Jewish and Christian tradition, but also towards a new way of speaking about God, a way that is not incredible in the face of the victims of our violent history.

The American-Jewish art historian Carol Zemel suggests the possibility of the memory of Auschwitz shedding new light instead of just obscurity – no matter how precarious this may be.[18] She studied the work of photographers who recorded life in the East-European Jewish ghettos of the 1930's. Roman Vishniac, with his famous book of photographs, *A Vanished World*, is the most famous name she mentions. Originally, Zemel's reconstructions with these photographs were meant for the eyes of modern American Jews. They could be proud that they no longer belonged to – as Zemel calls it – these 'doomed people' who had no other way out of their misery than the practice of 'extreme piety'. However, after Auschwitz, according to Zemel, we can no longer look at Vishniac's photographs in that way. To us now, they are attempts to shed a light on people unseen.[19] Those that had at first been mere figures in a world that had finally lost its relevance, because of modern progress, after the Shoah became regarded as people who had pinned their hopes on something other than modern progress with its emphasis on strength and success.

The memory of Auschwitz appears to do something similar to the religious and theological tradition. After Auschwitz, faith can never again hold fast to the divine truth, but instead appears as the hope for something other than what is offered by modern progress. Speaking about God, theology makes no sense as an attempt to acquire speculative and indisputable knowledge about God that has not been tainted by history. However, it does make sense as a conversation on the road of hope, as a conversation along the way about what is done and experienced from hope. A Christian identity can only mean devotion to the search for the meaning of the Christian tradition and, in particular, that of the history of Jesus of Nazareth.[20]

---

[17] D.J. Fasching, *o.c.*, 42-43, 104.

[18] I only found an interview with Zemel by Saskia Klaassen (Herinneringen aan onmodern leven. Anders kijken naar foto's van uitgeroeid joods leven, in: *Mare. Leids Universitair Weekblad*, May 4th 1995, 7), on occasion of the lecture she had given in Leiden.

[19] See the title of the book edited by Marion Wiesel, *To Give Them Light. The Legacy of Roman Vishniac*, New York 1993.

Hope

In Fasching's view, Christians should allow themselves to be advised by what Jewish thinkers have been saying about Jewish identity after Auschwitz. Elie Wiesel puts it as follows: 'The essence of being Jewish is: never give up – never surrender to desperation.' He quotes an aphorism by Voltaire: 'When all hope has vanished, death becomes a duty', but believes that this is not true for Jews. 'When all hope has vanished, Jews will invent new hope. Even amidst desperation, we try to justify hope.'[21] According to Wiesel, when all hope has disappeared, hope becomes a duty, and taking on that duty is what constitutes Jewish identity.

As with the Jewish writer, M.S. Arnoni, who similarly accepts the task of having to keep on searching for the meaning of the death of his murdered mother as a survivor of the great horror. As long as he has not found this meaning, as long as the behavioural patterns that made Auschwitz possible still exist, Arnoni does not want any rest, not even in his death. He wants his death, as he puts it with a gripping, literally breathtaking prophetic pathos, to harbour 'all attainable secret symbolism' that connects it with the fate of the victims.

> No tears may be shed, like no tears were shed when they died, in a hole in the floor of a ghetto or in a concrete mass execution chamber. No funeral procession, no ceremony, no flowers, no visitors, no condolences. Nothing. Although I would like all of it.[22]

For me, Irving Greenberg shows what incredible, unimaginable hope lies hidden in this behaviour. In a way that even exceeds the boundaries of what is considered to be good taste – but is there any other way of speaking about God after Auschwitz? – he connects the images of God's presence from the book of Exodus with what happened in the death camps. He further suggests

---

[20] Paul M. van Buren (*A Theology of the Jewish-Christian Reality*. 1: *Discerning the Way*, San Francisco 1980, 13-17) speaks – also in connection with the issue of dealing with Auschwitz – of theology in terms of 'talk as we walk'. In the same context, F. Marquardt (*Von Elend und Heimsuchung der Theologie. Prolegomena zur Dogmatik*, München 1988, 166-262), be it much more technical and elaborate, speaks of 'evangelical halacha': unlocking that road of God's commandments with the eye, while you are on it.

[21] E. Wiesel, *A Jew Today*, New York 1979, 194; 196.

[22] M.S. Arnoni, *Moeder was niet thuis voor haar begrafenis. Verslag van een reis door een verloren vaderland - Een overlevende van Auschwitz-Birkenau terug in Polen*, Amsterdam 1984 (originally 1980), 304.

the impossible possibility that the cloud of smoke of burned bodies during the day and the pillar of fire from the crematoria at night show the way to a new form of community and humanity in which Auschwitz will become forever impossible.[23] For the moment, we can do nothing but remain on duty while the horrors proceed.

These statements of Wiesel, Arnoni and Greenberg – and of other survivors – are convincing, because they have been affected by the shoah. Nothing would damage their testimony more than light-hearted appropriation of it by a gentile. That is not what I set out to do in this chapter, although many readers will say I have repeatedly been on the edge of the precipice.[24] What is at stake here is that the Jewish testimonies, in all their inimitability, show a new way in which human identity can be shaped. A way that is consistent with a clear approach that I also perceive in the Christian tradition, and which tells us to find our own identity in relationship with the victims and sufferers. 'Who is weak, and I am not weak? Who is offended, and I burn not?' as Paul puts it programmatically to the Christians of Corinth. 'For when I am weak, then am I strong' (2 Cor. 11:29; 12:10). As far as I am concerned, this is a powerful exhortation to find my identity, not in a strong idea on what should be done, thought and believed, but in my being moved by the world as it is and the extent to which it makes me an alien to any clear, powerful determination of identity. I will have to be satisfied with the knowledge that who and what I am is at stake, and with the expectation that my hope for a different liberation than that promised by modern progress, is not in vain.

This may seem vague, but I do mean something concrete. This can be understood from a photograph that appeared in the newspapers on 19 January 1996: a day earlier, fire had been set to an asylum seekers' centre in the German city of Lübeck, probably by one of the inhabitants, and at least ten people had died. The photograph shows the gutted house and a black woman, her arms spread in desperation and appeal, screaming in pain and anger about what had happened, showing us how terrible it is, and impatiently waiting for a time when these things will never happen again. To me, she is the embodiment of choetzpah, and in the footsteps of the men in the fiery furnace from the book of Daniel, she calls on the sun and the moon, the heat and the cold, the heavens and earth, to praise God. Nevertheless, she fully realises that for now, this is not happening, and that the dewladen breeze has again failed to blow when it was needed.

---

[23] I. Greenberg, 'Cloud of Smoke, Pillar of Fire', 55.

[24] Fasching sometimes comes close to the edge too; See A. van Harskamp, God en het kwaad van Auschwitz, in: A. van Harskamp (ed.), *Geloof en vertrouwen na Auschwitz*, 11-30.

Through the Eyes of the Other

Towards a Feminist Revision of Christology

Manuela Kalsky

> "Christology is like a bowl of spaghetti,
> you take one string and the whole mass begins to move."
> *Mercy Amba Oduyoye*

Introduction

This remark by the Ghanaian theologian Mercy Amba Oduyoye fascinated me. It not only shows the complexity of questions regarding Christology, the doctrine of Christ, but it also challenges us to answer the question: What does it mean when 'the whole mass begins to move'? What are the implications of this shift? Will it be a threat to our certainties and identity?

Christology is like a bowl of spaghetti. Each string has its own function in a whole that is difficult to keep in an overall view. The 'whole mass' threatens to fall apart into separate strings when this logic of unity is at stake. The theological structure is a complex one. There is no redemption without the fall, no resurrection without crucifixion, no longing for a new heaven and a new earth without suffering. An apparently organic whole, in which the entanglement of the strings seems to suggest a complexity that renders the following warning almost superfluous: Do not touch it. Do not tinker with Christology; do not tinker with the heart of Christian faith. After all, what is at stake here is nothing less than what makes 'spaghetti' a 'spaghetti'.

Despite all more or less explicit warnings, female theologians have started revising Christology from a feminist perspective. They have begun picking up string by string. Indeed, the Christological mass has started to move. Many women see this as a liberating disentanglement of an oppressive unity instead of as a threat to their Christian identity. As far back as 1973, Mary Daly consistently criticised the oppressive aspects for women of accepted Christology in her book, *Beyond God the Father*. She concluded that the unique incarnation of God in the shape of a man is sexist and legitimises the oppression of women. She considered the focus on the sacrificial death of Jesus in Christian religion to be necrophilia and merely promoting the traditional role of the self-sacrificing woman. Mary Daly could find no salvation for women in Christianity, and decided to take the post-Christian way. She exposed the doctrine of Jesus Christ as discriminating towards women. Cracks began to appear in the 'grand Christian narrative of redemption'.¹

If at first, the focus was mainly on exposing the aspects of Christology that were oppressive of women, it is now slowly moving towards a reconstruction of Christology from a feminist point of view. Starting with the historical experiences of women, the question is asked anew: what do evil and salvation mean to women in their specific contexts? The term 'historical experiences' indicates that this does not merely concern the individual experiences of women. These cannot be separated from the socio-political context in which they develop. However, these experiences of women came about in a patriarchal culture, which has not just influenced everything around them, but has also profoundly shaped the experiences, identity and the habits of thought of women themselves. The 'hermeneutics of suspicion' should not just be applied to Christologies developed by men;² feminist models also need a suspicious and self-critical analysis.

Elizabeth Schüssler Fiorenza introduces the term 'Athena complex' as a heuristic category for this kind of analysis.³ She refers to Greek mythology in which the goddess Athena is not borne by her mother Metis, but from the head of her father Zeus. This origin myth of Athena, who is known as the archetype of wisdom, shows that feminist theologians have to prove themselves, according to Schüssler Fiorenza, as daughters of their fathers. Seemingly without a mother, they spring from the thought of an Almighty father.

As a heuristic category – that is, as a criterion for searching, rather than as a moral category – the 'Athena complex' can also be helpful in a revision of Christology. It commands a self-critical answer to the question of the extent to which feminist-christological concepts have been influenced by the theological presuppositions of the 'Fathers' and thereby indicates an epistemological problem. Thus the question can be raised about why the manhood of the saviour has been so central to the feminist-theological discussion. The official Vatican Document 'Vatican Declaration on the Question of the Admission of Women to the Ministerial Priesthood', published in 1976, gave rise to this question, as it declared that

---

[1] For a feminist perspective of the 'theology of the cross', see: R. Strobel, Feministische Kritik an traditionellen Kreuzestheologien in: D. Strahm, R. Strobel (eds), *Vom Verlangen nach Heilwerden. Christologie aus feministisch-theologischer Sicht*, Fribourg 1991, 52-64; C. Janssen, B. Joswig (eds), *Erinnern und aufstehen – antworten auf Kreuzestheologien*, Mainz 2000.

[2] For the theoretical elaboration of this feminist hermeneutics see: E. Schüssler Fiorenza, *Bread not Stone. The Challenge of Biblical Interpretation*, Boston 1984.

[3] E. Schüssler Fiorenza, Der "Athenakomplex" in der theologischen Frauenforschung, in: D. Sölle (ed.), *Für Gerechtigkeit streiten. Theologie im Alltag einer bedrohten Welt*, Gütersloh 1994, 103-116.

women cannot become priests, because they cannot show a physical resemblance with the saviour. Rosemary Radford Ruether reacted with the question: 'Can a male saviour be the saviour of women?' From the beginning, this question had a rhetorical character.[4] Without actually dealing either with the problematic nature of Jesus' manhood or with the underlying issue of a possibly irreducible difference between men and women, the question was answered in the affirmative. A male saviour can be the saviour of women because many feminist theologians, particularly those with a liberation theological perspective, believe that the issue is not the manhood of Jesus, but his humanity, which is intended for the salvation of all. After all, Jesus did not just die for men, he is the saviour of all humankind, including women. However, if most feminist theologians are not really troubled by the man Jesus, why is this question asked in the first place? Perhaps Schüssler Fiorenza is right when she says that feminist theologians, like good daughters, are trying to solve their fathers' problems concerning Christology, by developing a Christology which has degenerated into a Christolatry? On reflection, should we conclude that our questions are often those of our 'fathers', and that we, albeit unconsciously, continue their tradition? Are the questions fe-minist theologians have so far posed to Christology really their *own* questions? If they are not, then what should their questions be?

Apart from emphasising the self-critical approach of feminist christological models, the 'Athena complex' also shows the necessity of seeking what women call salvation and liberation in everyday reality. It challenges a 'creative imagination'. The revisions following from this are founded on a wholesome suspicion that has to maintain the tension between breaking down and rebuilding, between scepticism and creative imagination, searching for different symbols, a language, new texts and new communities.

In this article I hope to present the various phases of the feminist christological discussion, in order to demonstrate that the current feminist revision of Christology must be closely related to a revision of its epistemological presuppositions. The reader will be confronted with various themes that have also been discussed by postmodern philosophers: the end of 'the great narratives', a review of the accepted epistemology, the questions concerning unity and plurality, uniformity and variety. Initially, I will not engage in a discussion with postmodern thinkers. This is not because it would not be meaningful, but because I want to show that these so-called postmodern questions have not been forced upon feminist theologians from the

[4] R. Radford Ruether, *To Change the World. Christology and Cultural Criticism*, London 1981, 45-56.

outside, but that they gradually present themselves from the inside as a radicalisation of our own modern ideal of emancipation. In the first part of this article, I will discuss the problem of uniqueness and identity, then the tension between context and relational plurality will be discussed. The christological statements of the Korean theologian Chung Hyun Kyung will serve as an example of this. Finally I deal with the hermeneutical challenge these different ideas about salvation and evil pose to any discourse about Christology.

Uniqueness and Identity

In 1971, Leonard Swidler published an article in which he called Jesus the first feminist.[5] He describes Jesus as the first non-chauvinist man, who achieved a clean break with the chauvinist structures of his native Jewish culture. Hanna Wolf also shared this view and painted Jesus from a depth psychological perspective as the androgynous human being; as the one who succeeded in uniting the male and female sides in his person.[6] Both concluded that Jesus had not been sexist; he was 'entirely different' from other members of his sex in a patriarchal context.

Initially, women applauded these 'discoveries'. Biblical stories were interpreted against this background of Jesus' unique relation to women. This made it possible to use the bible to show that the source of Christian faith was not intrinsically oppressive of women. Women wanted to show that it was worthwhile to follow a different path to Mary Daly since her point of view implied an inevitable break with the Christian tradition. Mary Daly herself reacted quite laconically to Swidler's discovery that Jesus was supposed to have been a feminist: 'Fine. Wonderful – But even if he wasn't, I am!' Daly's criticism is clear. She rejects any attempt to project modern feminist ideals on the past and to subsequently legitimise them in the person of Jesus of Nazareth. Her criticism is not primarily aimed at the man from Nazareth but rather at the *Wirkungsgeschichte* that through its emphasis on the uniqueness of this man has led to the idolization of manhood.

It is noteworthy that the first christological attempts from a feminist perspective – apart from Daly's – are strongly related to traditional concepts of Jesus Christ. Apparently, it was clear to some feminists what 'Christology' was, is and should be. It was something that went without saying, that need not be discussed. Questions and answers all revolved

---

[5] L. Swidler, Jesus was a Feminist, in: *Catholic World*, 212 (1971), 177-183.
[6] H. Wolff, *Jesus der Mann. Die Gestalt Jesu in tiefenpsychologischer Sicht*, Stuttgart 1979.

around the person of Jesus, around *his* meaning and *his* uniqueness. Wolf's concept of the androgynous man, and Swidler's feminist Jesus were quite simply attempts to show Jesus as he really was. Not the dogmatic Christ, but the historical Jesus, was the point of interest for feminist theology.

Their attempts remind us of the *Leben Jesu Forschung* (Quest for the Historical Jesus) of the nineteenth century. In his work 'The Quest of the Historical Jesus', Albert Schweitzer has shown that the various images of Jesus were projections of the authors, rather than the reconstruction of historical facts. From an historical-critical perspective, the *Leben Jesu Forschung* was seen as a failure, because it presented the subjective desires of the various authors instead of the expected objective historical facts and biographical details about the life of Jesus of Nazareth. In fact, Schweitzer himself does not condemn these 'fantasies', he rather points out the necessity and the positive strength of the contextual character of *every* interpretation of Jesus.

> Thus each successive epoch of theology found its own thoughts in Jesus; that was, indeed, the only way in which it could make Him live. But, it was not only each epoch that found its reflection in Jesus; each individual created Him in accordance with his own character. There is no historical task which so reveals a man's true self as the writing of a Life of Jesus. No vital force comes into the figure unless a man breathes into it all the hate or all the love of which he is capable. The stronger the love, or the stronger the hate, the more life-like is the figure which is produced. For hate as well as love can write a Life of Jesus, and the greatest of them are written with hate: that of Reimarus, the Wolfenbüttel Fragmentist, and that of David Friedrich Strauss. It was not so much hate of the Person of Jesus as of the supernatural nimbus with which it was so easy to surround Him, and with which He had in fact been surrounded. They were eager to picture Him as truly and purely human, to strip from Him the robes of splendour with which He had been apparelled, and clothe Him once more with the coarse garments in which He had walked in Galilee. And their hate sharpened their historical insight. They advanced the study of the subject more than all the others put together. But for the offence which they gave, the science of historical theology would not have stood where it does today.[7]

The authors of the *Leben Jesu Forschung* and the authors of feminist theology have a number of things in common. Feminist theologians wanted to free Jesus from this same supernatural aura. They wanted to free Jesus from the 'patriarchal halo' that underpins the exclusion of women from the priesthood and is used to keep women as second-class citizens in both

---

[7] A. Schweitzer, *The Quest of the Historical Jesus. A Critical Study of Its Progress from Reimarus to Wrede,* London 1998, 4-5.

church and society. They wanted to show that Jesus' contact with women had not been hierarchical and patriarchal but based on equality. For the sake of the emancipation of women Jesus had to become one of *them*: they created him after their own image and he became *their* liberator, notwithstanding that he belonged to a different sex and religion. This discovery of his unique contact with women had an apologetic function towards their own Christian feminist identity. As with the *Leben Jesu Forschung* of the nineteenth century, this picture of Jesus was relatively short-lived. The image of the feminist Jesus ended in failure because it did not live up to the ethical standards of feminist theology itself – a standard that demanded practical justice and liberation for *all* women.

Others, in this case Jewish women, showed that the image of Jesus as the liberator of women contained anti-Judaistic tendencies.[8] As with the various strands of traditional theology, Jesus was separated from his Jewish context in these feminist theological publications. An ideal was effectively constructed which revived old prejudices and myths. The old way of thinking in terms of contrasts which Rosemary Radford Ruether had warned about in her book *Faith and Fratricide* (1975) re-surfaced. On the one hand, Judaism was depicted as wicked and thoroughly patriarchal while, on the other hand, Christianity was presented as new and liberating for women. Women, following in the footsteps of their fathers, were searching for their own feminist theological identity. Following the traditional pattern, this was done by excluding 'the others' and at the expense of Jewish women.

The problem of this anti-Judaism in feminist theology has not yet become past history, although there is a general willingness among feminist theologians to distance themselves from an anti-Jewish interpretation of Christology.

Some years ago the American-Jewish feminist Susannah Heschel, in the German magazine *Publik Forum,* accused feminist theologians of anti-Judaism.[9] Heschel is of the opinion that Jesus is still represented in a way

---

[8] On the problem of Anti-Judaism in feminist theology see: J. Plaskow, Anti-Judaism in Feminist Christian Interpretation, in: E. Schüssler Fiorenza (ed.), *Searching the Scriptures. A Feminist Introduction,* New York 1993; K. von Kellenbach, *Anti-Judaism in Feminist Religious Writings,* Philadelphia 1994. For the German discussion see M. Therese Wacker, Feminist Theology and Anti-Judaism. The Status of the Problem in the Federal Republic of Germany, in: *Journal of Feminist Studies in Religion* 7 (1991) 2, 109-116.

[9] *Publik Forum,* nr.1, Jan. 15th 1993, 26-27. See also S. Heschel, Jüdisch-feministische Theologie und Antijudaismus in christlich-feministischer Theologie, in: L. Siegele Wenschkewitz (ed.), *Verdrängte Vergangenheit, die uns bedrängt. Feministische Theologie in der Verantwortung für die Geschichte,* München 1988, 54-103.

in which his role as a liberator of women is in strong contrast with the patriarchal structures of Judaism. In addition to the commentaries of various feminist theologians on Heschel's thesis, part of an article by Elizabeth Moltmann-Wendel was printed, entitled 'Jesus, the Taboos and the New'. In this text, Moltmann-Wendel defends the idea that not everything that is regarded as a 'difference' between Judaism and Christianity should be interpreted as anti-Judaistic. She argues that it is important to continue emphasizing what is new in Jesus and in the Jesus movement. She believes that the Jesus movement is in keeping with the prophetic tradition and critical of Levitical codes of purity. In the story of the woman who had a problem with bleeding for twelve years (Mk 5:25-34) she sees evidence that Jesus broke with these purity codes. This break, she argues, illustrates traces of an autonomous female form of life. Moltmann-Wendel writes:

> From the perspective of Christian men and women in early Christianity and many Christian women right up to the present age, Jesus has really brought something new. The 'new' is always new in contrast to my old experience of living under coercion, in a lack of freedom, by laws and imperatives. The fact that 'Judaism' often had to represent the 'old' in a very generalised way in Christian theology, is a regrettable mistake, which has produced anti-Judaism again and again. The 'new' can be used arrogantly against the 'old' in traditional contrastive thinking. However, it can also be seen as something differentiating and alternating, as a new space and a new time, as something, which opens up a new existence. If we no longer want the experiences of 'the new' in Christianity, we will not get anywhere beyond Christian ethics. – The Christian 'new' that we have to see in our case, is a trace of an autonomous female form of life.[10]

In what follows I will not dwell on the general accusation of anti-Judaism directed against Moltmann-Wendel. However, I do want to engage in a self-critical analysis of the epistemology used by her and other feminist theologians. I believe that our way of trying to find feminist Christian identity has to do with the problem of reproducing mechanisms of exclusion. I use Moltmann-Wendel's text as an example, to make clear why this process of identity building is, in my opinion, the wrong way to go.

Moltmann-Wendel does not want to play off the 'old' against the 'new', but nevertheless she does. She uses the 'concept of difference' in a negative way. Her search for identity is still contrasting 'us' against 'the other' rather than trying to find an identity via relationships in which differences are respected and enjoyed. She wants to guarantee the vitality of her own

---

[10] *Publik Forum*, 27.

movement, but fails to notice that this is achieved at the expense of turning another approach, the Jewish tradition, into a lifeless one. 'The others' become inanimate, although they are actually rooted in a living tradition and are perfectly able to speak. To Moltmann-Wendel, this speaking is not the starting point for the difference between Judaism and Christianity. It is not the dialogue and the meeting, the collective exchange and reflection on a possible cooperation with Jewish women, that offers to provide a definitive answer. Nor does she pose questions about the contemporary experiences of Jewish women, about their Jewish practices today, and specifically about the function of purification rituals, such as the *mikwe*, which is still being practised and has actually been rediscovered by Jewish women. All this fails to contribute towards determining the difference. The exchange of contemporary experiences of Jewish and Christian women about the issues of menstruation or impurity is not central for her. Rather, what is new is that which she projects as 'new' onto the Jesus movement of the first century. Moltmann-Wendel talks about a new era, a new space and a new existence, but she does not find the 'new' in the present, but rather in the wandering Jesus movement of two thousand years ago. She thus uses the concept of difference apologetically instead of communicatively. In her search for the 'new' in Jesus she reproduces a traditional epistemology, based on a division between subject and object, between 'we' and 'the other'.[11] I believe Moltmann-Wendel defends the Christian identity of the 'fathers' when she uses this contrastive way of thinking.

However, if this is not the way to proceed, the question as to how a feminist theological identity should or can be realised, remains open. It seems to me that one must *search for* feminist theological identity in the future, *inspired* by the stories from the bible, and that one should not try to *find* it in the past, using those stories as a *legitimisation*. I think the latter inevitably means the reproduction of a traditional Christian way of thinking, namely, the confirmation of personal identity at the expense of others. Their voices are not heard, and they become objects, that are at the mercy of the projections of the subject.

The fervent longing for freedom and a space, where life is good to women, points to the future. It is of an eschatological nature and therefore still developing. It cannot surface like a treasure from the past. The negative demarcation towards the other obstructs the search for an inter-subjective identity in which the different visions of salvation that women have become visible both within and outside the Christian tradition. This

---

[11] It is amazing to have to come to this conclusion because Moltmann-Wendel focuses firmly on relationships in her quest for new theological roads within the Christian tradition.

would mean that a different epistemology that makes it possible to see 'others' as truly 'other' is required. The 'other' will then no longer be reduced to an extension of myself and need no longer be in line with my own projected norm. In short, this way of searching for identity requires maintaining the opacity,[12] the non-transparency of the other.[13]

This presupposes a break from the predominant logic about the determination of identity. Jesus can also remain the other without the need to meet our ideals. He does not have to be a feminist or an androgynous being that conquers the differences between the sexes. He can remain the Jewish man from Galilee, whom we do not know via biographical traditions but through stories. These stories have a certain rhetorical intent, which can contain both oppressive and liberating elements for women, as Elisabeth Schüssler-Fiorenza clearly shows in her book *But She Said*.[14]

However, these biblical images and expectations of salvation, written predominantly by men, should not remain the only object of feminist criticism. They should also retain their critical function both towards stories of evil and salvation for women. However, they should shed their exclusive and normative status. Instead, they can stand alongside the concepts of salvation that women had and retain. Only then can these stories exist with critical authority. The latter will remain the 'other' stories and will not be appropriated by us. I believe it is important to maintain this critical tension

---

[12] Theo Witvliet borrows this concept from the black religious scholar Charles Long. He uses 'opacity' in connection with the black historical experience. He shows the reverse side of the Enlightenment from the perspective of the colonised peoples. The colonial view did not only have an impact on them from without. The 'epistemic violence' (Gayatri Spivak) to which they were subjected influenced and distorted also their perception of themselves. See Th. Witvliet, *The Way of the Black Messiah*, London 1987, 186-189; Ch. Long, *Significans, Symbols and Images in the Interpretation of Religion*, Philadelphia 1986; S. Harasym (ed.), *G.C. Spivak. The Post-Colonial Critic. Interviews, Strategies, Dialogues*, New York 1990.

[13] In her book *Longing for the Fall*, the Dutch theologian Annelies van Heijst raises also objections against a way of thinking that focuses on relationships but still rejects the 'radical otherness'. She prefers to see distance, separation and autonomy as aspects of relationships and not as their antithesis. She reaches the conclusion: 'That which is other and the other person can never be entirely known or understood. This reservation on an epistemological level is, however, not a relational reservation: not knowing completely does not have to stand in the way of a relation. In hermeneutical terms, difference-in-relation presupposes an understanding, the basic attitude of which inclines more towards discontinuity than an echoing recognition, where recognition is not entirely absent.' In this way she arrives at the concept of an 'ethic of lasting difference'. A. van Heijst, *Longing for the Fall*, Kampen 1992, 191-192.

[14] See E. Schüssler Fiorenza, *But she said. Feminist Practices of Biblical Interpretation*, Boston 1992.

between the stories in the bible and the stories of women and men today, to make sure we do not end up with romanticized stories of women as the *locus theologicus*. These will remain the starting point for feminist theology but this will always be accompanied by the awareness that they cannot express pure womanhood because they are constructed. They also need a hermeneutics of suspicion as I tried to explain at the beginning of this article by means of the example of the 'Athena complex'.[15]

But before this necessary self-critical reflection on 'the experiences of women' can take place, experiences and visions of salvation and evil ought to be named. Until now, these feminist visions of salvation have not functioned in our speaking about the sacred. The words 'But Mary kept all these things and pondered them in her heart,' (Luke 2:19) lead Carol Christ to state that:

> *Her word* never became flesh and dwelt among us. Perhaps no one ever asked her what she was thinking. Perhaps she never heard stories which could give her words for her own experience. Perhaps the man who wrote the gospel narrative simply could not imagine what it felt like to be in her position. Whatever the reason, her experience and the experiences of other women have not shaped the sacred stories of the Bible.[16]

To be able to find the words and the stories of evil and salvation of women today the French philosopher Luce Irigaray proposes the inverse movement to that described in the Prologue of the gospel of John with the words 'and the Word was made flesh'. It should now read 'and the flesh was made word'.[17] The latter expresses the quest for what women experience as salvation from the wisdom of their bodies. It seems to me to be of even greater importance that we do not neglect what it actually reads in the Prologue to the gospel of John "and the Word was made flesh, and dwelt among us". When I strategically inverse this statement in line with Irigaray, it reads: Women dwell here and their flesh becomes word, – many words, for women live in many different places. The contextual location does not just pose the question of the sexual difference, and with that the difference between the representations of salvation and evil by women and

---

[15] See also A. van Heijst, *Longing for the Fall,* 170f.

[16] C. Christ, Spiritual Quest and Women's Experience, in: C. Christ, J. Plaskow (eds), *Womanspirit Rising. A Feminist Reader in Religion*, San Francisco 1979, 230.

[17] On the discussion of theology and female subjectivity, see A.C. Mulder, *Divine Flesh, Embodied Word. Incarnation as a Hermeneutical Key to a Feminist Theologian's Reading of Luce Irigaray's Work*, Utrecht 2000; J. Hopkins, *Towards a Feminist Christology,* Kampen 1995, 81-97; G.M. Jantzen, *Becoming Divine. Towards a Feminist Philosophy of Religion,* Manchester 1998, 77-99.

men, as Irigaray intends, but it also respects the cultural differences between women, which are also part of their reality. I would like to demonstrate how the Christ-event is relocated in the particularity of these places, by means of the christological statements of the Korean theologian Chung Hyun Kyung.

Contextuality and Relational Plurality

Chung situates her christological images in an Asian context. Asia is the birthplace of all the great religions of the world. 58% of the world's population lives in Asia and the largest part of these are Hindus, Buddhists, Muslims, Taoists and Confucians. Only 3% is Christian. Economic poverty and cultural riches are often found in the same place. Chung caused quite a stir with her attitude at the conference of the World Council of Churches in Canberra when she invoked the Spirit of those that had been wronged in history. She called upon the spirits of Hagar, Uria, Jefta's daughter, Jeanne d'Arc and many others who had become the victims of colonialism, fascism, racism and sexism; people who paid the ultimate price in their fight for the freedom of their people – like Mahatma Gandhi, Steve Biko, Oscar Romero and the students in Tiannamen square. She called upon the spirit of the exploited earth and of the polluted air. Her list ended with a call upon the spirit of Jesus: 'Come, spirit of the liberator, our brother Jesus, who was tortured and killed on the cross.'

Chung explained that people in Korea believe that those who have died an unjust death, become *han*-spirits. It is the responsibility of the survivors to listen to these *han*-spirits and redress the injustice that has been done to these people. According to Chung, these *han*-spirits are the icons of the Holy Spirit and their function is to make the voice of the Holy Spirit heard. This is how they show us the path leading away from the forces of death – away from the ideals of progress, from the compulsion to possess, from envy and dissension – to the road of creation, to the safe keeping and liberation of life. Following the Korean Minjung theologian Suh Kwang Sun, Chung calls this the 'political economy of life'. In this economy mutual relationship and not individualism is the most important value. Here we do not find an anthropocentric vision of the world and a dualism of body and spirit or nature and culture. Rather, its foundation lies in relationality, which is the source of life. The emphasis lies on the connectedness of humanity and cosmos.

The image Chung associates with this attitude and the work of the Holy Spirit stems from the popular religion of East Asian women and is embodied in the goddess of wisdom and safety – *Kwan In*. *Kwan In* is a *bodhisattva* or an enlightened being. She could enter nirvana unhindered, but instead voluntarily chooses to stay on earth, out of solidarity with everything that is suffering and for the purpose of bringing it to enlightenment. Her wisdom is healing and she gives all living things the strength to swim to the shore of nirvana. She will wait until the entire cosmos, people, birds, trees, air and water have been enlightened, to finally live together in nirvana in eternal wisdom and safety. Could this image, Chung asks, be a female image of Christ, the firstborn who precedes all others and takes others along?

The hermeneutical starting point for Chung, and, as she sees it, also the end of her hermeneutical circle, are the historical experiences of Asian Minjung-women in the Korean context.[18] Chung's hermeneutical steps lead through a critical awareness which exposes the ideology of oppression to a critical selection which women from various religious traditions and political ideologies experience as liberating and important. The selective use of texts from different traditions, including the Old and New testaments, is also part of this hermeneutics. She describes it as follows:

> I do not try to articulate Korean women's God-experience from biblical or orthodox theological perspectives in a traditional sense. Instead I like to name Korean women's experience within our cultural context of suffering and lifegiving using our traditional symbols and metaphors in an organic way. Then I try to make connections between Korean women's experiences and the Christian tradition.[19]

Most women in Korea are not Christians and therefore do not express their longing for liberation from oppression in terms of Christian symbols. In her search for a liberating theology Chung also uses non-Christian symbols and rituals that she finds in the life stories of these Korean women. This way, the stories of her two mothers – the woman who gave birth to her and

---

[18] By saying that women are at the same time the starting point and the end of the hermeneutical circle, Chung underlines that every hermeneutics is contextual and biased so that one perceives the particular effect of posing norms that results from it as well. She does not suggest the existence of a seemingly universally valid hermeneutical circle. This raises the problem where the moment of criticism with regard to the female experience can appear and where the place is to be found for a critical reflection on oneself. See Chung Hyun Kyung, Han-pu-ri: Doing Theology from Korean Women's Perspective, in: V. Fabella (ed.), *We dare to dream. Doing Theology as Asian Women*, Maryknoll, New York 1989, 144; id., *The Struggle to be the Sun Again. Introducing Asian Women's Theology*, Maryknoll, New York 1990.

[19] See idem, Han-pu-ri, 136.

the woman whom Chung did not know until recently, the woman who raised her – became sources for Christology.

In her article 'Following Naked Dancing and Long Dreaming', she analyses the situation of these two women – their social, personal and religious status, the things they have in common and their differences.[20] Chung does not classify these experiences nor does she try to force the frame of reference of socio-theological research on them. She tells these stories in a reflective way while trying to identify with the women in the story. In doing so, she is writing their *social biography*.[21] The narrative aspect is central and her direct involvement makes biography and theology flow into each other without cancelling each other out. In this quest, through the stories of their mothers, the oral tradition of the community of women, Shamans assume an important position. Chung writes:

> Shamans are strong women, 'organic intellectuals', wounded healers, exorcists, household therapists, singers, dancers, comedians, actresses - beautiful, attractive and sensual women. They are best known, however, as *priestesses* who become *mediators between the living and the dead*. In the communities of Shamanistic *Minjung*, they have no church buildings or hierarchical, clerical structures among themselves. Shamans treat people in their home or their client's home. There are no strict, orthodox texts in Shamanism.[22]

Women shamans help Minjung-women in healing their mental and bodily suffering and transform their brokenness. Like *Kwan In* these shamans are a female image of Christ for Chung.[23] She compares the transformation of

---

[20] Id., Following Naked Dancing and Long Dreaming, in: L.M. Russell, Kwok Pui-lan (eds), *Inheriting Our Mothers' Gardens. Feminist Theology in Third World Perspective*, Philadelphia 1988, 54-72.

[21] The Korean Minjung theologian Kim Young Bok has given to this narrative method the name of 'socio-biography'. According to him, this socio-biography reveals the hidden reality. See K. Young Bok, The Problem of Women and Socio-biography of Minjung, in: *The Task of Korean Women's Theology*, Seoul Korean Association of Women Theologians (KATW), Seoul 1983, 78-92.

[22] C. Hyun Kyung, Opium or the Seed for Revolution? Shamanism: Women Centred Popular Religiosity in Korea, in: *Concilium* (1988), nr 199, 103.

[23] In his article 'Does Christ Have a Place in Asia?', Aloysius Pieris refers to an image of an Asian Christa he came across in one of Chung's publications. It shows a female Shaman on a cross placed on a lotus flower. She has a sword in one hand and a bowl of rice in the other. Her breast is bare, ready to feed. Pieris compares the bare breast with the stabbed side of the crucified Jesus from which there was a flow of the water of the Spirit. As far as I know Chung does not mention this image in any of her publications. See A. Pieris, Does Christ Have a Place in Asia? A Panoramic View, in: *Concilium* (1993), nr 2, 40-41.

the *han* by the shaman with the acts of Jesus, who exorcised evil spirits and cured the sick and possessed.

According to this thinking, the dogmatic, abstract questions concerning the unity of the church, of the singularity of Jesus, the authority of the bible or the ecclesiastical tradition are not important. These are not normative for a theology that needs to be developed; what is important is the life-giving spirituality that offers Korean women an opportunity to reclaim their humanity for themselves. This is the standard for a liberating theology of women in the Asian context, and it is, according to Chung, what the various religions have to satisfy. Biblical stories and other sources of religious tradition are only meaningful when they serve the life-giving force of liberation (Han-pu-ri). A theology that does not account for the everyday physical and spiritual lives of women in Asia, is an inadequate theology for Asia. A relevant theology must be able to disentangle the *han* of Asian women and liberate them from oppressive elements within their own culture.

Is this not syncretism, the mixing of elements from different traditions, asked many Western theologians after Chung's appearance in Canberra. However, she has no such qualms. On the contrary, she considers syncretism to be an enrichment. In her opinion, anything that serves life and contributes to the liberation from oppression is in accordance with Christian faith. Chung calls on the wisdom of her mothers, whom she calls syncretists, in the positive sense of the word. They have eclectically drawn from different religious sources and have thus created 'a religious cosmos in their hearts'. They have always sought that which could give their life strength, and they have allowed themselves to be guided by this knowledge. Because of this, neither Jesus, nor Buddha, nor Confucius, nor any other sage has ever become the centre of their spirituality. At certain times these played an important role in their lives. However, the real centre of their spirituality was life itself and consciously or unconsciously, they kept looking for the life-giving aspects in the various religions and rejected their destructive forces.

Chung calls this spirituality of her mothers a 'syncretism aimed at survival and liberation'. This spirituality requires a different way of knowing. What the broken bodies of these women tell us is a new starting point for Christological epistemology. This is why Chung says 'We are the text' and, from this materiality of life stories, her search for new symbols starts. The bible and the Christian context are a collective Jewish and Christian memory, which may be important through the 'dialogical representation' (Kwok Pui-lan) and should not be neglected, but they are not seen as the exclusive sources of divine revelation. According to Chung the vitality of divine revelation cannot be confined to a biblical canon. After all, God did not come to Asia with the first missionaries. Long before Jesus was born divine revelation had manifested itself in Asia. This implicitly shows that Jesus cannot be regarded as the only incarnation of God. Chung assumes a continuing revelation and, therefore, even today God's text is written in the bodies of Asian women, in their daily struggle for survival, borne by their shaman spirituality of Han-pu-ri.

For Chung too, the search for messianic salvation for women in the Asian context is necessarily connected with a plea for a new way of thinking and with it a new vision of the other. She wants a practically oriented, contextual epistemology instead of an abstractly formulated dogmatic doctrine. As a critical liberation theologian she situates her 'epistemology of the broken bodies' in the liberating praxis of the oppressed and marginalized. This requires active listening, a critical analysis of society and a theological reflection on the everyday stories of women, which carry a hidden wisdom, which broadens the logic of the word and reason with that of the body.[24] Physical experiences are explored as a different form of knowledge and lead to the naming of the divine. This is how the word is made flesh in a specific context.

Whether it is the image Kwan In, the goddess of wisdom and safety; the shaman life-giving spirituality; the Christa as a crucified woman; biblical wisdom (Sophia); the matriarch Eku from Africa or the biblical image of Hagar, the revision and naming of concrete representations of evil and salvation from a female perspective in different cultures is still developing.[25] Neither the dogmatic questions of the Council of Chalcedon (451) about the nature of Christ, nor the question of the relation between the 'historical Jesus' and the 'Christ of faith' are an indication of the orientation of these christological subjects.

No longer is there *one* personified figure of salvation at the centre of things as a unique revelation of God. Instead, incarnation takes place where the *praxis of relational particularity and cooperation* is oriented towards a liberating syncretism.[26] To phrase it differently: it takes place whe-

---

[24] See M. Field Belenky, B. McVicker Clinchy (eds), *Women's Ways of Knowing. The Development of Self, Voice, and Mind,* New York 1986.

[25] For a survey on Christology from the perspective of women in different cultures, see D. Strahm, *Vom Rand in die Mitte. Christologie aus der Sicht von Frauen in Asien, Afrika und Lateinamerika,* Luzern 1997; M. Kalsky, *Christaphanien. Die Re-Vision der Christologie aus der Sicht von Frauen in unterschiedlichen Kulturen,* Gütersloh 2000; L. Isherwood, *Introducing Feminist Christologies,* London 2001.

[26] C. Heyward, *Speaking of Christ. A Lesbian Feminist Voice,* New York 1989, 21.

re dialogical imaginative power takes place, pursuing the messianic longing for becoming whole.

Christaphanies

The rediscovery of the differences among women and between women and men turns the unity of humankind as it was envisioned in the project of emancipation of the Enlightenment into a problem. Neither is the universal meaning of Christology any longer self-evident. This discovery brought about plurality and fragmentation.

I have tried to show that postmodernity is not some sort of game, forced upon us by French intellectuals, but that the questions of postmodern thinkers are phenomena of our Western culture and social reality. These postmodern questions are deeply rooted in modernity. In his book *The Inhuman: Reflections on Time* Lyotard writes:

> (...) the postmodern is always implied in the modern because of the fact that modernity, modern temporality, comprises in itself an impulsion to exceed itself into a state other than itself. And not only to exceed itself in that way, but to resolve itself into a sort of ultimate stability, such for example as is aimed at by the utopian project, but also by the straightforward political project implied in the grand narratives of emancipation. Modernity is constitutionally and ceaselessly pregnant with its postmodernity.[27]

Postmodernity as the offspring of modern culture reacts against it and at the same time radicalises its ideals. 'Post' should therefore not be regarded as a temporal 'after' modernity, but rather as a search from within, in which breaks and continuity with traditions demand a room for something new, with all the attendant ambivalences.

I would like to use the term 'Christaphanies', manifestations of Christa, to indicate the multitude of expectations and representations of salvation in different cultures.[28] The introduction of this concept serves a strategic purpose. It is not an attempt to develop a new systematic theological Christology from a feminist perspective. Rather, it will expose the multicultural diversity of personal, concrete experiences of women of salvation and liberation. Christaphanies are open to the past and at the same time directed towards the future. They allow for the ambivalences that are part of a revision of Christology from a feminist theological perspective. On the

---

[27] J.-F. Lyotard, *The Inhuman. Reflections on Time*, Cambridge 1991, 25.
[28] See M. Kalsky, *Christaphanien*, 303-329.

one hand, there is the continuity in the search for salvation, as it has taken place in Jewish and Christian traditions. On the other hand, there is discontinuity and suspicion towards a Christian tradition in which masculine representations of salvation have been used against women. Apart from this critical analytical side and the related hermeneutics of suspicion, Christaphanies also bring out a playful, creative side, which invites creative imagination in the framework of the hermeneutics of a creative actualisation: flexible, procedural and intent on relating.

Christaphanies represent multi-colouredness and can therefore not be reduced to the logics of *sameness*. The encounter of women from different cultures and the communication about contextual Christaphanies is paramount, precisely to prevent the creation of new absolute and specific representations of salvation.[29] Moments of divine truth and the possibility of an intrinsic determination of the interpretation of Christ are to be found in the encounter with other types of experiences, rather than in claims to the truth that have been made right from the start.[30] This encounter does not take place with the aim of creating a synthesis of the various positions. Rather than theoretical harmony, practical 'dissonance' will break open the familiar epistemological habit of thought and create new possibilities for a form of knowledge focussed on relations.[31] The crossroads of these different personal experiences and their socio-political analysis show up the oppressive structures and open up a possibility for a new understanding of universality as an *interactive universality*.[32]

The search for an interactive universality remains necessary, because the ethical demand for the liberation of women worldwide can only continue to exist as a feminist utopia and a self-critical moment if the interactive universality is not abandoned at the expense of particularity. The retreat into particularity means accepting that the differences between black and white, men and women, West and East, North and South are unbridge-

---

[29] In her book *The Wisdom of Fools* the English theologian Mary Grey uses the concept 'Epiphanies of connectedness' to emphasize the connectedness with the whole creation. According to her relationship is an ontological reality and thus an ΄epiphany of divine communication' that can restore the 'broken heartedness' (Rita Nakashima Brock) of the world. In how far this theology of relationship can accept really a room for dissonance in communication is a question that still waits for an answer. M. Grey, *The Wisdom of Fools. Seeking Revelation for Today,* London 1993, 60-66.

[30] See S.D. Welch, *Communities of Resistance and Solidarity. A Feminist Theology of Liberation,* Maryknoll, New York 1985, 15-31.

[31] See R. Braidotti, *Patterns of Dissonance. A Study of Women and Contemporary Philosophy,* Cambridge 1991.

[32] See S. Benhabib, The Generalized and the Concrete Other. Visions of the Autonomous Self, in: *Praxis International* 5 (1986) 4, 402-424.

able. However, as a result of this retreat we may lose track of the grand narrative of the liberation of all women. Difference without relationality, without a communicative ethics, without a common longing for a Messianic age, leads to political impotence. Stopping the search for a new understanding of universality would mean giving up the ethical appeal to global political responsibility. So far, feminist theologians have not been prepared to abandon the ethical imperative of liberation for all women.

Not the fictitious dialogue but the real encounter is the condition for an interactive universality. The everyday reality of women and critical reflection on that reality from a social and cultural point of view, individual life stories and social biography, desires and longing for salvation, are the themes for this encounter in which the differences in sex, race, culture, sexuality, class etc. are being thematised. Initially, this means finding new forms of communication to be able to really hear each other in the sharing of another reality. This can be done by trying to see through the eyes of the other, by reversing roles, by playing with different identities, by shifting our perspective to widen our contextually limited view. The ultimate goal of all this is to recognise as messianic only that which meets the ethical demands of the good life for all. Women from the 'third world' especially have pointed out that verbal communication and rational knowledge alone are not enough to bring out the wisdom of women. Poetry, literature, dance, art and popular culture are discovered as new sources for this way of knowing.

Christological truths that express both a break and continuity with Christian tradition are revealed in the everyday social reality of women from different cultures. In outline, new ways and revelations of salvation become visible. In my opinion the great challenge we are faced with is not just enduring this fragmented nature of christological content instead of *one* dogmatic doctrine, but also the related search for Christian identity as a project of communication. The break with a functional and objectifying view of *the other* requires a radical change of the personal perspective and with it a different epistemology. This changing of the rules for christological discourse will no doubt cause uncertainty, but it also creates a space for the search for a multicultural feminist theological identity.

The Greatness of a Little Narrative

Reflections on a Powerless Christian Identity

Ad Willems

Introduction

What am I to do when I begin writing about Christian identity? Should I read something like Adolf von Harnack's *Das Wesen des Christentum* (The Essence of Christianity), or maybe 'Changes in the Concept of Church in the last Twenty Centuries'? However, the question does not engage my interest in quite that way.

I do realise that questions of identity are very important. They are, clearly, not 'academic' questions. As structures, frameworks, political parties and churches crumble, questions like 'who am I?'; 'who are we?; and 'what do we actually still engage with?', will be asked more often and will be more potent existentially. Questions about meaning usually refer in essence to personal lives. Even if the question as such is not asked that directly, it still seems reasonable to associate a number of expressions of aggression and depression, of dismay and despair in our society, with the question of identity. What at first seemed a highly personal and individual question suddenly appears to be the question: 'Where do I belong?'

When the question is rephrased in that way, then it is also my question. This is something I would be prepared to write about. I will not attempt to provide a fresh or definitive answer to the question about the essence of Christianity. I will review and reflect upon the road that I have travelled as a Christian and as a theologian. For me this road was the development of my identity. This awareness is not always equally manifest, but I will try to explain this in the course of my article. At the same time, I know that there have been a couple of major breaks on that road. I also know that I have experienced these breaks together with many other people at the same time. People's historical and biographical development rarely ever runs in a straight line. The current period can be characterized by a rapidly increased awareness of those breaks. This intensifies the quest for one's identity and deeply affects the carefree trust in one's own perspective. At the end of this reflection, as becomes evident, I find myself amidst the break and the fragments with a powerless narrative of Jesus. It is exactly his powerlessness which gives this narrative a new impetus.

Pitfalls

As stated, this is going to be a reflection with some autobiographical elements. As I am convinced that my experiences were also the experiences of many of my contemporaries, I can write about them in terms that are more general. For the sake of clarity, I need to first emphasise the importance of the 'problem of identity' before I continue.

First, I am interested in the question of the singularity of *Christian believers* precisely as believers. Of course, believers are faced with questions of identity in other fields too, particularly in the emotional and social fields, but I will leave these fields for the moment.

Next, I will address the question of the identity of believers *as a community*, in other words, the question of the identity of the church. But let me qualify this further: I am interested in the singularity of the community of Christians rather than the specific singularity of Roman Catholics, Reformed or Protestant churches. A more general, deeper group identity connects the personal identities of many types of believers.

As soon as such a question about (group) identity is explicitly asked, there is a danger that one starts looking for an *immutable* singularity. This is not just a recent tendency. It is actually a heritage of Aristotelian and scholastic philosophy that managed to obtain a foothold in theology. I still remember my first philosophy teacher. He told us about the ancient philosopher Heraclite (c 500 BC) who stated that everything is in a constant process of change (*panta rhei*). Next, and with some sense of drama, he introduced Aristotle (c 350 BC) who asked himself whether that was actually possible. After all, things change but they also stay the same? If this were not the case, something completely new would arise all the time. Thus, the idea came about that there was a constant and immutable 'essence' of things beneath all the changes. Changes only took place in the inessentials ('accidents') that were carried by the 'essence'. This is also how human existence was regarded. Her/his 'essence' was undying and universal, but 'accidents' like size, colour, strength, wisdom or virtue could change over the years and was different between individuals. The philosophical question *par excellence* would now be the question about the description of this essence. Changes were only circumstantial. Medieval scholastic philosophy has largely adopted this approach to reality. In ethical discussions about the beginning and the end of human life, these ideas still play a role: when does the 'essence' of man come into being and when does it end?

In reflections on what it is to be human, the idea about such an 'metaphysical' or 'a-historical' singularity has been eclipsed by the awareness of the fundamental historicity of man and the world. That historicity – much to the dislike of church authorities – cleared the way for the conviction that the faith of people is also an historical reality rather than a substance that is chemically pure and stainless, passed on in time. Such a positioning means distancing oneself from all forms of fundamentalist understandings of the self by the faithful. For now, I briefly conclude – I will have to return to it later – that the question of the identity of the community of believers focuses our attention on the peculiar *combination* of continuity, breaks and renewal.

One other misconception needs to be noted beforehand. This is the idea that identity is always and in every respect 'exclusive'. Here again I will limit myself to the question of group identity. Sociologists show us what we already more or less consciously know: people who form a group display a number of common characteristics. Although the churches sometimes resist this, even they cannot escape sociological laws and they therefore display a number of characteristics that they have in common with other groups as well.

However, quite apart from these general characteristics there are several specific characteristics and even goals that churches can have in common with other groups. A number of the ideals of political groups and institutions of care, trade unions, welfare organisations and environmental organisations, Amnesty International and Greenpeace – to name but a few – are also ideals with the communities of Christian believers. This stands to reason. As Christians in this age we share the experience of a number of contrasts. The benefits of technology and automation contrast palpably with the well-being of many. Environmental pollution, disease and the problems of unemployment do not stop at the church door. That is why 'the church' can justly be characterised as a 'contrast community' or a 'counter institution'.[1] However, this characteristic does not determine the singularity of the community of believers. It means that we oppose certain excrescences of modernity and persons and institutions that, consciously or unconsciously, defend these harmful consequences ('exclusive') together with others ('inclusive').

The particular identity of each group is formed by one fundamental option that embodies itself in the course of history through many derivative characteristics, each of which can also appear in other groups. The existence of alliances that do not lead to fusions illustrates the possibility of a coexistence of particular identity with inclusivity.

---

[1] See G. Lohfink, *Wie hat Jesus Gemeinde gewollt?*, Freiburg 1982, 142-170; J. De Kesel, *Omwille van zijn Naam*, Kampen 1994.

Connecting to a Life Story

The shared basic conception of Christian faith is to choose the (continually renewed) story of Jesus of Nazareth. By now it should be clear that such a statement obviously does not exclude the possibility and the value of any other non-Christian faiths. Happily, other forms of faith do exist. Nowadays we encounter them more often. Yet, here I feel the need to express what in my opinion is that common basic option for Christian faith. That story itself consists of several stories. These tell us about a Jew who has lived and died in such a way that there were people who, upon hearing this story, 'found something in it'. This narrative continues to our day, and there are still people who find 'salvation' in that story. This is why they 'accept' it. This means: they try to arrange their own lives in accordance with the way Jesus showed them. His life story is prolonged in the life stories of those that accept it as an inspiration for their own lives.

This story is, however, not self-evident and does not create an unbroken identity. It is not self-evident because it did not create evidence, a verifiable certainty that the acceptance of that story would give everybody's life meaning, no matter what the circumstances are, neither at the time when it happened, nor in our time. Then, and now, it requires a *conscious decision of faith* that will 'prove' its soundness for all time – a tree is known by its fruit! The decision cannot be enforced from evidence.

Nor does the story create an unbroken identity for those who accept it. Some fragments of my own life story as a believer and a theologian will serve to illustrate this point. To neutralise this slightly embarrassing aspect, one could read a different name for mine. I am thinking of the story of Jacques Pohier as he described it in his book about breaks in our conception of God.[2] He was born in the same year as me, became a Dominican and underwent the changes in our culture over the last few decades in a way that is strikingly similar to me.

Looking back I see that history as a continuity-in-breaks. Where others might mainly see the breaks, I actually do see continuity. My 'self' was the substratum beneath the sometimes profound changes. In the years before the Second World War, I 'heard' the story of Jesus of Nazareth – as Pohier did – as something that was self-evident. In the climate of an urban popular Catholicism that story was an all-encompassing system that determined the coordinates of my (=our) life through practices in our family, the friars that taught me, and the practices of my church. During and immediately after the war, I chose (naturally within those coordinates) to commence training as a priest with the Dominicans. This involved no struggle and hardly any

---

[2] J. Pohier, *God in Fragments*, New York 1986.

sense of vocation, even though the decision to go to a boarding school at the age of thirteen was quite a psychological change. After that adjustment joining the Order of the Dominicans seemed a more or less logical acme. From 1946, the six-year course in philosophy and theology also took place in an atmosphere of unbroken continuity, notably that of the Roman Catholic Church and its prevailing Thomistic tradition.

Breaks in the Story

Nevertheless, in those first years after the war, in which French existentialism spread, a shift occurred that heralded the first break. The attention for timeless essences, in which Thomism excelled, shifted to a reflection on human existence. Theologians like Karl Rahner also became sensitive to the *historicity* of human existence in general and therefore also for faithful existence. Could unchanging dogmas be integrated with the human condition? Catholic dogmaticians who made this question their own liked to disguise themselves as historians to avoid measures by the doctrinal authorities within their churches. In various studies they showed that conceptions (like dogmas) and practises (like sacraments) that were held to be immutable sometimes had a turbulent history. In due course, 'doctrine' also proved to be a historical and therefore changing theological system. This may seem a somewhat terse and dry description, but the accompanying break that also occurred in the monastic superstructure of my 'ordinary' life was far from minor. If everything is historical, does that also hold true for the dogmas about God and Jesus Christ? What about the Church: was it perhaps not the rock-solid (Mt. 16:18) and unchanging domain of God? That would mean however that there were no more unchanging 'essences' within that church: the rules governing church life could adapt to the demands of time and a concrete institution like monastic life, with its stable 'apartheid' compared to the transitory world would only be an historical and, in that sense also coincidental, manifestation of Christian faith. Why hold on to all kinds of traditional patterns like *horarium*, habit, hairstyles, community formation and living?

The continued effect of the discovery of historicity in everyday life had many characteristics of a crisis for Pohier and many of his contemporaries including myself. In my case this was amplified even further by the gradual breakthrough of what I will call for the sake of brevit, the philosophy of the Enlightenment. As theologians such as Piet Schoonenberg and Edward Schillebeeckx illustrated, God and man were not in competition, and this awareness came to express that man did not have to relinquish his or her *autonomy* in faith. Anything that entered your life as normative from the outside could or rather should justify itself first in front of the forum of reason. In order not to deliver your life to an incomprehensible authority, every authority, which included the church and even the 'divine', had to be able to justify itself and thus let go of its claim to purely formal authority. It will come as no surprise that contact with church authorities (who were not yet that 'enlightened') and a divinely authoritative Bible – including the story of Jesus of Nazareth – became highly problematic.

The infiltration of the *postmodern* condition has only gradually come about in me. This is hardly surprising considering the emotional shockwaves that the consequences of modern philosophy caused. The things one has gained, with so much effort, in the premodern church are not easily relinquished. Nevertheless, the detrimental aspects of modernity were soon apparent. Social isolation and professionalisation turned out to be the darker drawbacks of emancipation and technical progress. What conclusions should be drawn from this? The word 'postmodernity' was buzzing everywhere. The things that presented themselves under the umbrella of 'postmodernity' did not always appeal to me. It all seemed so disparate. I read Milan Kundera's *The Unbearable Lightness of Being* with genuine surprise. Some time later enthused stories of younger colleagues about the 'end of all great narratives' did touch a chord, but they also posed many questions. Do little narratives replace every form of great narrative? If so, is communication still possible, or can everyone just limit themselves to their own 'little' narrative? Does the abuse of reason legitimise its abolition? At the same time, beneath these questions, a feeling grew that what I had discovered in the modern age (an awareness of historicity and autonomy) was on the one hand radicalised and, on the other, had become a problem. But this needs further explanation.

First I need to explain this 'radicalisation'. This refers to the experience of historicity mentioned earlier. What started out as an exciting demythologisation of ancient dogmas and church practices that, to this point, were considered to be unchanging, led to the realisation of a general subordination to the conditions of finite existence. Did that make existence any 'lighter'? At first I did not experience this. Yet after a while it began to dawn on me that all our attempts at transcending our own contingency were doomed to end in failure. As usual, the Germans have a splendid word for this: *Kontingenzbewältigung* (dealing with contingency), as if our finite situation is like that of a wild animal needing to be tamed. Still, there is no escaping that we have not always existed; our current existence is coincidental; we might just as well not have existed; we will not be around forever. My Christian faith has long served as an attempt to escape my radical finitude. Only quite lately did I discover that I had been playing into Richard Rorty's hands. After all, he is convinced that attempts at *Kontingenzbewältigung* are the main task theologians and metaphysicians have set for themselves. I now believe that theologians should not allow this task to be forced upon them.[3]

Whereas my awareness of historicity was radicalised, postmodernity has actually put the ideal of the autonomy of Enlightenment into perspective for me. What happened there? The subjects liberated from oppression each received their sovereign little island that had their own strict parameters. Outsiders and strangers were only admitted after they had rid themselves of all their strangeness. Gradually I realised that the appearance of the 'other' does not just mean the threat of alienation but also a challenge to the adventure of 'being-different-together'. However, this challenge could no longer be experienced completely. Reason's purges had removed all strangers and others. This is when it dawned on me that that *ratio* was the degeneration of a much broader human capacity. Only the spirit incarnated in body and emotion can respect the 'otherness' of the 'other' and even become fascinated by it.

Healing Fragments

The old shared frame of reference of popular Catholicism was in tatters. Could it still bring people happiness? If the context of the story of Jesus has been so thoroughly changed by modernity and postmodernity then what can this story of the man from Nazareth still mean for salvation? I am relieved to notice that the question for Christian identity formulated thus far is not as stifling as it sometimes used to be. The question itself and the fragmented answers have become more bearable and lighter. I consider that development to be a good thing in itself. I no longer feel the need to provide a severe 'generally valid' answer. It is now all about a simple establishment of my choices within the coincidental coordinates of my time and place in the history I share with others. That history coincidentally (just because I was born here) brought me into contact with that story. Upon reflection, I realise that the story has been told and interpreted repeatedly even before it reached me. The same thing happens in my own life. I ask myself whether there has been a constant factor amidst all these changes. I am thinking of the origin of the story. There is the man from Nazareth and the little group of people that saw 'salvation' in him at the time and appar-

---

[3] R. Rorty, *Contingency, Irony and Solidarity*, Cambridge 1989, 23-38.

ently found it hard not to speak about it (Acts 4:20), such that they formed a group – something like a 'church'.

What happens when I am confronted with the stories about this man across all the breaks in history? I am no longer confronted with a 'great' narrative of universal import that forces itself upon me. Previously – in my own childhood – that was still the case, even though I only realised it in retrospect. In the meantime the churches have lost their institutional influence in Western Europe. Confessional organisations feel embarrassed when asked for their Christian foundation. In education and care for the sick, the sisters, deaconesses, brothers and friars, have almost disappeared. Christianity has lost its natural character that it used to have in large parts of our society.

The form of the story itself is also changing drastically. Until recently it still gave rise to substantial systematisations and well conceived syntheses, in which theologians accounted for their profession and gave it its universal validity *via* a scientific model. Nowadays they prefer essays. The narrative character of theology is now played against abstract systemisations. To academic colleagues of other faculties in the Netherlands, this has been a reason to deny theologians their place within the university. Ministries that administer the budget are all of a sudden interested. It is now clear however that the Constantinian turn that at some point achieved the dominance of the churches and became an important factor in public life is now vanishing at a rapid pace in Western Europe. We could mourn this fragmentation but the sound of people who experienced that previous 'great' narrative as forced upon them, as a violation and humiliation, can be clearly heard. Unmistakably, the painful experiences of women can be clearly heard as well. Postmodern sounds, proposed by J-F Lyotard, have broadened the awareness of liberation.

> Too quickly do we forget that the Christian uniform vision has led to all sorts of terror or has at least allowed itself to be used for it. The relentless hunt for heretics in 'Christian' Antiquities and the Middle Ages, the Western European delusion of witchcraft, the bloody wars of religion, religious intolerance, the crusades, the *conquista*, the fierce fight of the magisterium against dissent, democratisation and plurality in the church and theology, statements like 'Gott mit uns', 'God save the Queen' and 'God bless America' are all phenomena that can be explained from a strong totalitarian vision of Christianity. In other words, the religious narrative about meaning has too often violated all experiences of meaninglessness, everything that does not fit the wonderful framework![4]

---

[4] R. Burggraeve, Christendom en postmoderniteit: Doemdenken, heil of bescheiden kansen?, in: *Collationes* 23 (1993), 29.

If the great narrative was only fragmented then we could still look at the fragments. Not for the purpose of sticking them back together and displaying them in a museum but because the fragments themselves contain more inspiration than the great narrative that has been unmasked as totalitarian. Some of these fragments actually resist attempts, which would later prove successful, to forge them together into one unified powerful narrative. An attentive observer, who manages to ignore the general human need for self-affirmation and the formation of power, may even wonder how the life stories of Jesus managed to lead to such massive ideologies. Jesus' parables, but also many of his other words and especially his deeds clearly reject a royal Messianism, a concentration on his person or the exercise of power and riches. The gospel of Mark records with endearing faith how difficult this was to understand for the disciples (Mk 4:13; 8:21.33; 9:32; 10:37). It does require a rare reversal to regard poor widows, slaves, children and 'the last' as role models. This is deservedly seen as 'paradoxical ethics'. In the end, it is obviously even more paradoxical that a man who is executed by the authorities in the prime of his life through a legal procedure should initiate a movement that would guide people for twenty centuries. Is this perhaps due to the totalitarian forms this concrete, powerless narrative adopted through the ages?

This seems improbable to me. There is no dictatorship that has held out for many centuries purely through coercion and discipline. There were always counter stories in the margin of the great narrative with its heavy unchanging dogmas that have kept Christianity alive. Through the ages, more and more people stopped appealing to 'the' tradition. This is true of innovators (who were later recognized as such) like Benedict, Francis, Dominic, Martin Luther, Teresa of Avila, Dietrich Bonhoeffer, Jacques Gaillot and Elizabeth Schüssler Fiorenza. However, the vitality of the story of Jesus of Nazareth was just as much guaranteed by innumerable life stories of those who may not have been part of its 'mainstream' history. Therefore, they did not leave their mark on 'the' tradition. However, in their concrete lives, they did show that the old and enduring story of the man from Nazareth was able to repeatedly spring to life again in their age. Their lives may not have been contrasting counter stories, but they do often provide a mildly ironic paraphrase on the declarations of the high and mighty. Their sometimes quickly forgotten acts can also be said to be an attempt to relive the life of Jesus in their days. In doing so, they realised what Schillebeeckx formulated as a condition for life or even perhaps a dogma: 'The present that is always new becomes part and parcel of re-determining the past'

A Lighter Story of Jesus

How does 'regaining the past in a creative way' work? The American theologian-exegete Marcus Borg showed this in the way he interpreted the story of Jesus.[5] He described the dissatisfaction with the dogmatic standard story he was brought up with. After a number of fundamental 'breaks', and several years later, he started to rediscover the history of the Jew from Nazareth. In that rediscovery his own dissatisfaction and the achievements of other exegetes and historians, such as E.P. Sanders and J.D. Crossan, played an important role.[6] It gradually appeared that the life story of Jesus, which had so clearly been situated in time and place, could offer him considerably more orientation than the great canonical narrative of the established churches. The paradox in Borg's rediscovery of Jesus' life story is striking. Not the dogmatised message of redemption from a god-man, but the testament of the searching Jesus of Nazareth, who even develops into an alternative prophet in the footsteps of John the Baptist and now turns out to be able to grant people new life.

Looking back on my own development I find the same paradox. The little personal narrative has provided the original vitality which the great unmasked narrative had hidden. This was achieved without any major upsets, in the same way as the narrative, that grew into an ideology, still managed to contain traces that referred back to the defenceless little narrative it all started from. I will leave aside whether this historical 'beginning' can still be traced, and if so, how that can be done. Not just since Albert Schweitzer (1875-1965), but also with Rudolf Bultmann (1884-1976), so much has happened that an attitude of complete scepticism is now superseded. To insure that we do not become stuck in the historical and hermeneutical questions involved, I will first try to indicate the elements of the story of Jesus that appear to me to be crucial for our present Christian identity. This is not just inevitable, I actually intend to allow the 'new present' that Schillebeeckx talked about to have its say in 're-determining the past'. I am interested in the aspects in Jesus' life story that, for me, correlate with questions of existence as they present themselves to me, here and now, and about which I have tried to indicate their origin.

As I write this I feel compelled to separate these aspects of Jesus' life. At the same time I am painfully aware of the fact that it concerns an exis-

---

[5] M.J. Borg, *Meeting Jesus Again for the First Time*, San Francisco 1994.
[6] See J.P. Meier, *A Marginal Jew: Rethinking the Historical Jesus*, New York 1991; E. P. Sanders, *Jesus and Judaism*, London 1985; J.D. Crossan, *The Historical Jesus. The Life of a Mediterranean Jewish Peasant*, Edinburgh 1991; Id., *Jesus. A Revolutionary Biography*, Philadelphia 1994.

tential event, in which the different aspects have a simultaneity that is essential, though it can never be adequately communicated. This life, as it has been lived, cannot be grasped conceptually. This is true of everybody's life, so it must be true of Jesus' life as well. The elements I intend are: Jesus' familiarity with what I would like to call 'the ground of our collective existence' which is inseparably connected with his total commitment to others (his *diakonia*, see Mk 10:45). This latter element has been ignored too often in history.

Nowadays the way that familiarity with the ground of our existence is formulated in the stories of the bible, and any observations derived from it, raises many emotional questions, particularly for women. This concerns what is called Jesus' 'Abba-experience', that is, his experience of God as a father. Even his prayer, that Christians all over the world use, is known as the Lord's Prayer. Precisely because this expresses Jesus' familiarity and emotional bond with the father, it seems obvious that gender specific emotions will play a role within the patriarchal structure. I feel unable to respond to that in an adequate way. I will therefore limit myself to an attempt to describe what I think is at stake in this element of the story of Jesus.

From exegesis and historical research we get the impression of a pious Jewish man, to whom the faith of his ancestors was a source of an authentically committed life. His education in 'the Law and the Prophets' had taught him the deep religious realisation that the God of his ancestors was also 'his' God. This realisation struck him as it so often did with the people of his time. The dream from which someone like that lives is not the effect of their own efforts, but the fruit of openness, receptiveness, 'active passivity'. This had happened to many prophets in Israel. Their God had made Himself 'known' to them.

With Jesus this brought about an experience of faith together with a self-evident intimacy. The character of that closeness was expressed in words that seemed obvious from daily experience. His God was 'fatherly and motherly love' to him (E. Schillebeeckx). That is why he could use the word 'Abba' to speak about his God with the casualness of a child. This natural closeness reminded the Jews of the stories about their prophetic arch-ancestor Moses who had, according to the Torah, been an almost daily conversation partner with the Eternal. They regularly heard this continuing contact being described in the synagogues: 'And the Lord spoke to Moses face to face, as a man speaks with his friend.' In the story of Moses, this miraculous closeness does not diminish the equally deeply rooted sense of the *mystery* of the Eternal. This even created a verbal paradox: 'And he said, Thou canst not see my face: for there shall no man see me, and live.' (Ex. 33:11.20; Deut. 34:11).

Jesus' first disciples had a similar experience. His 'Abba' experience was an experience of such closeness that Jesus would characterise it with such peculiar phrases as 'All things are delivered unto me of my Father' and 'I am in the Father, and the Father is in me' (Mt. 11:27; Jn 14:11). At the same time, however, they also took note of his testimony: 'my Father is greater than I' (Jn 14:28). This had also been recognised in Jesus' vision that determined his entire life, the convergence of the intimacy with the source of life and the simultaneous reverence for the all-transcending mystery that it involved.

The Temptation

Fascinated by Jesus' intimacy with 'the Father', people nevertheless soon had problems with the other pole of his 'Abba'-experience. In particular the combination of intimate closeness and simultaneous reverence for the all-transcending mystery of the 'Other', which confronted the disciples who, however, did not share this immediate experience themselves, posed a real problem. This became clear already in the first generation after Jesus' death. Mark the evangelist did not shrink from ending the story of Jesus' death dramatically – this end of the world for his loyal disciples – with Jesus' exclamation 'My God, my God, why hast thou forsaken me?' (Mk 15:34) The quotation from the Psalm 22:2 may well have served to put the desperation over the end of this life within a scriptural framework, that is, as by the divine will. After all, many knew the much more hopeful continuation of the psalm quoted. Nevertheless, the choice of this verse, in the face of death, does show traces of a shared fear of the fathomless mystery of God as the unrelenting Other. Luke apparently had qualms about this verse. He chose a different quote from the scriptures that was less shocking. 'Father, into thy hands I commend my spirit' (Lk. 23:46; Ps. 31:6). This brought the end of Jesus' life in harmony with that familiarity with the Father, which had been so clear during the rest of Jesus' life.

The differences in interpretation, that are already shown in the canonical gospels, are only a prologue to what was going to happen later. Jesus' closeness to the Father took on metaphysical proportions. The focus soon shifted to the divine-human composition of his person. The fact that this man had been focussed on self-transcending and doing the will of the Father, by virtue of his closeness to the mysterious source of all life, eventually faded into the background. Christian believers may well have found it easier to cope with the veneration of a god-man than with following a Jewish man. This explains the warning: 'Not everyone that saith unto me,

Lord, Lord, shall enter into the kingdom of heaven; but he that doeth the will of my Father which is in heaven.' (Mt. 7:21; Jn 4:34; 6:38).

No matter how understandable the temptation to concentrate solely on the wondrous closeness of Jesus' connection with God, the other component of his attitude to life was just as 'essential'. Still, the fixation on his self-evident closeness to the Father gained the upper hand. It even led to a device that would be used as a standard for Christian orthodoxy. An obtrusive great narrative developed. With it a 'perversity', a reversal of the actual issue, took place, and still does today.

> A theoretical specification of the divine event that overwhelms Jesus, and forms the meaning and the heart of his life, corrupts this event, and therefore verges on heretical, one-sided misrepresentation.[7]

The essence of Jesus' life was not a devout sojourn with the Father. He did pray (Mk 1:35; 6:46) and sometimes he rejoiced in spirit (Lk. 10:21). However, his intimacy with the Father essentially included the awareness of God's otherness. *That is why the other side of the 'Abba'-experience was the mission to and actual effort for the 'others' on earth.* The Other *par excellence* directed Jesus to the publicans and sinners (Mk 2:14-17). He considered it his calling to seek and save what was lost (Lk. 19:10). The weak and the small attracted his special attention because the heavenly Father does not want any to be lost (Mk 10:13-16; Mt. 18:14). The positive view about 'strangers' was also put in that perspective (Lk. 4:21-30). Giving them space and, therefore, a new life, was what made the 'Kingdom of God' closer through Jesus' works. That 'king-dom' was to become a new type of society.

To their dismay that desired society sometime took on such new forms that even the first disciples too could not comprehend it (Mk 6:52; 8:16-17; 8:32-33; 9:34). There would be no ruling, just serving (Mk 10:42-43); in order to save your life, you had to lose it (Mk 8:35). Jesus' true, healing attention for others was the outstanding embodiment of his encounter with the Other. The all-transcending secret of that Other was the secret of *all* life and, therefore, at the same time fascinatingly close. Jesus did not speak about a metaphysical God. He told stories and lived his life. He referred disciples to his own acts when they asked him to show them the Father of life. Those that see me act, see the secret of God's justice at work (Jn 14:8-10).

What only slowly dawned on the disciples was considered a threat to the subtle order of society by one of the influential groups in Jerusalem. To

---

[7] E. Schillebeeckx, *Jesus. An Experiment in Christology*, New York 1979.

them, righteousness with God was identical to ritual purity. That purity coincided with distinctness. That is why the priest and the Levite had to pass the half-dead man on the other side (Lk. 10:30). Jesus broke through this xenophobia. He told them that God made the sun rise both over the good and the bad and that God's reign consists in finding the lost and that people can also be healed on the Sabbath. This way of life inevitably led to the ultimate consequence, for such an infringement of the sacred order could not be tolerated by a number of members of the Sanhedrin. Acceptance of death sealed Jesus' life in the mystery of God.

Imitation

It is the greatness of a little story of life, like that of Jesus, which does not force itself but calls for imitation. Such imitation means that one's own life story is developed in the light of that earlier story. Therefore, it will be a personal story, not a copy or imitation of the one that went before. One of the conditions for this is that it is lived with pleasure. It is not an obligatory story. Only those that see the 'salvific' prospects of this life will embark upon it.

It is part of the *plot* – the intrigue – of the story of Jesus' life, which is his shocking freedom as also a liberating freedom, where salvation comes to those who dare to trust themselves to the *mystery* of Jesus' life story. Somebody like that will in turn adopt the story of and about Jesus, tell it to others, and turn their own praxis of life into a repeated, yet new parable.[8]

The question now is whether the story of Jesus, stripped of its 'greatness', still has enough power of expression to give people a perspective, and with that, a personal identity in the current postmodern situation. The aim is not to form a private or exclusive group as such. The question is whether this story of Jesus has any perspective to offer to us within the co-ordinates of our present context. If people recognise and accept this, it will give them their own story and their own face. To continue rejoicing in this, people would come together every now and then to testify to this and 'celebrate'.

The reflection on the cultural situation of the here and now has made me realise, as I have suggested, the consequences of a number of experiences of breaks. An intensified awareness of our radical contingency and a threatening loss of 'the other' through the recovery of our own autonomy now determine our present context. It is obvious that the story of Jesus

---

[8] E. Schillebeeckx, *Evangelie verhalen*, Baarn 1982, 370.

does not provide ready-made answers to these constituents of the current understanding of life. A full life story never answers but occasionally inspires imitation. This happens when it describes situations that correlate with the situations of later listeners and readers and puts them into a new perspective. The coming about of this process can be strengthened or weakened by what that life story has brought about in the course of history. I believe that our perception of the power of expressiveness of Jesus' life story has been expensively compromised by the recurring ideologisation of it. However, for me it does regain its lustre because our current situation actually opens our eyes to those elements in that story that had faded into the background. To retrace these elements, exegetical studies and historical discoveries can no doubt be helpful but the testimony in word and deed of believers is more powerful.

They opened their eyes to the possibility of – while imitating Jesus – resigning themselves to the mystery of existence in active equanimity (*Gelassenheit*), as Eckhart often called it. That equanimity can model itself on the moments of simple surrender by Jesus to his 'Father'. His almost self-evident trust in God's closeness in daily life is reflected in the sometimes almost simple attitude to life of people who surrender to what life is offering them. Their lives have their mysteries too. One of the 'daily' mysteries is death. Through the ages, reading and knowing the story of Jesus has given people the courage to accept the inevitable otherness of death and with it their own finitude.

It once baffled me that the theologian and clergyman Friedrich Schleiermacher (1768-1834) in his earlier years already wondered why most believers want to be 'immortal'. He thought that was highly 'unreligious' and reminded his audience of the words: 'those who lose their life for my sake, will keep it, those who want to keep it, will lose it'.[9] On his deathbed thirty-five years later he celebrated the Lord's Supper with his intimate friends and bade them a peaceful farewell. It seems that the Jesus story can enlighten us. This opens up the possibility of accepting the strangeness of our life's end with a mixture of fear and intimacy. Is this perhaps what Bonhoeffer meant when, in the hour of his death, he wrote: *Das Jenseitige ist nicht das unendlich Ferne sondern das Nächste* (The transcendent is not the infinitely far but rather the most intimate).[10]

However, sometimes the otherness of death is so absurd that the word 'inevitability' dies on our lips. This mainly happens when it is clear that it

---

[9] F. Schleiermacher, *On Religion. Speeches to its Cultured Despisers*, Cambridge 1996, Speech II.
[10] D. Bonhoeffer, *Widerstand und Ergebung*, München (Siebenstern-Taschenbuch 1) 1964, 189.

involves not just the contingent human condition. When people are involved in violence and death, life demands more than simple 'acquiescence' but 'resistance'. It seems to me that Mark's story of Jesus' death, as I have described it, is a manifestation of that experience of absurdity. Jesus could only experience the early death-through-execution of the righteous as an ultimate question for God. The Other was no longer present. However, his followers kept believing in what Jesus had shown them in his life. After all, the other side of his close relationship with the Father was his orientation on the many 'others' around him.

From the nearness of the mystery of human existence, which had a familiar name for Jesus during his life, he received his mission to engage with the fate of many others. To Jesus, this mystery was reflected in the day to day faces, not just of those who had been robbed of their lives by the law of finitude, but also of those who had been robbed of their freedom by the violence of others: widows, the poor, strangers, the hungry, the thirsty and prisoners. In our situation, we could probably add several more categories to the story of Mt. 25:35-40. Jesus' mission was that he allowed himself to be challenged to be near all those people whose existence was threatened. He passed through our human, contingent existence, by giving communication, that is, new life to those who were in danger of dying before their time.

The identity of those who allow themselves to be inspired by the story of Jesus does not just consist of the 'mystical' component, but also an orientation towards others that goes with it. Imitation of Jesus in a group ('church') should aim to combine these two poles. Indeed, the intimate relationship with the Other is insufficient without a real effort for others. Liturgy and community with fellow believers needs to be combined with social care as a characteristic of authenticity. When believers no longer know where to look, Bonhoeffer can show them the way: *Das unendlich Ferne ist das Nächste* (The infinitely far is the most intimate).

Landing Stages for the Divine

A Correspondence on Transcendence and Everyday Life

Leo Oosterveen and Anne-Claire Mulder

Dear Anne-Claire,

God works in mysterious ways. At the same time as Dutch author, Geert Mak, in his best seller, describes how God has disappeared from Jorwerd, his small rural hometown, God, the divine, the transcendent seems to have made a strong comeback. Mak argues that God has been replaced by the ideal of planning, constructability and rationalisation prevalent throughout society. Personally, I feel that it is just as plausible to argue, more than ever before, that people are searching for something that transcends planning, constructability and rationality.

I feel that we are also in search of transcendence. Because questions such as these involve a very personal quest, writing letters can help us to discover how God and the divine managed to regain a place in our everyday lives. After all, perhaps the personal element involved in this quest will be better acknowledged through the most personal of all literary genres, the letter. Letters allow one to locate one's deepest personal motives and intuitions. For these reasons I thought it would be a good idea for us to start writing letters to each other about transcendence. I am doing this however in the hope that our letters will be more than just individual documents. I am actually hoping that our personal theological reflections will also help others in their search for recognisable and useful interpretations of the transcendent in their lives.

The close link between transcendence and everyday life is confirmed time and time again at the staff meetings we have at the *Dominican Study Centre for Theology and Society* on the topic of transcendence. If transcendence cannot be found in everyday life then where is it? Although, I must admit that I feel a bit awkward about the idea that transcendence can be found in everyday things. I will try to discover the reasons for this awkwardness by reflecting back on my past and trying to discover when and why transcendence disappeared from my life; when and why everyday life itself became a (stifling and hopeless) transcendence. What will be the contours of a renewed relationship between transcendence and everyday life for me today? In formulating this, I will occasionally link transcendence more to God, the divine and its representations, and occasionally more directly to experiences that are not, or need not be, directly related to God or the divine.

The Exodus of Transcendence from Everyday Life

In the summer of 1970, when I was sixteen years old and spent a week at an abbey, I read a book about meditation. The author, a Buddhist monk from Sri Lanka, wrote that the path of enlightenment implied renouncing all (false) certainties, including all credos, all doctrines and representations of faith embraced because of some authority or for other reasons. Credos are a very counterproductive basis, he warned his Christian readers. Credos keep people captive to representations that appear to be objective and true but are in fact false. In other words, they offer false certainties. The images of faith offer an objectified false reality, with 'God' and all other representations of the divine the most prominent. I remember thinking that this was an excellent book, and its message certainly did not fall on deaf ears. After all, in those days I was very keen to take in the fresh air of secularisation. The idea of ridding myself of obsolete, stale images of God appealed to me. I felt that this monk's plea put him among those other advocates of secularisation. What made it even more appealing was the fact that it was an exotic plea (coming from Sri Lanka) as well as a religiously motivated one. It did however leave me with some questions. I was still in search of a personal form of spirituality or religiosity and image of God. Although it was still very vague I did not feel that I should destroy the 'personal' element as soon as I had found it. Is it possible to set out on the religious path 'without any preconceptions', I asked myself. And what was to become of 'my' Christian tradition?

Later these questions became even more direct and pressing. I was a third-year student of theology and had recently joined the Dominican order. From one day to the next I was struck by the realisation that I could no longer 'simply' believe, or rather that believing was no longer a matter-of-course. The normal, day-to-day aspects of religious and monastic existence, such as lectures, the celebration of the Eucharist and attendance at daily offices, personal prayer, occupying yourself with your spirituality and the monastic life in a fairly open community. Indeed, the whole religious world I was living in suddenly became for me alien and meaningless. It seemed totally unnatural. I felt like a spectator to something and I knew I was no longer engaged. Faith, God and the sacred were no longer everyday things. On the one hand faith and spirituality and on the other everyday life had suddenly become completely detached. Everyday life was the real world; the religious world was a kind of make-believe world, a realm of spirits, though many religious practices were still part of my everyday life. Initially, I did not know how to handle this situation. I only gradually found a *modus vivendi* as a way of handling the situation. An interest in the critique of ideology and liberation theology, that had started to develop in the seventies, came to my rescue. These perspectives taught me that faith and the articulations of faith often seem beautiful and universal, but in fact can distract from the concrete struggle for liberation in everyday life or gloss over oppressive social contrasts. In that case faith has an alienating effect. On the other hand, if one were to follow this theology and choose to believe in a way that opened one's eyes to social injustice and the praxis of political liberation, faith would no longer be alienating. On the contrary, faith would then, as it were, forge a bridge between the prophetic promise of God's salvation and the struggle for our basic everyday existence. I don't know whether this new point of reference of mine did in fact do justice to the seriousness of my alienating experience or whether I was just simply trying to exorcise it.

In any event, oppressive experiences of faith alienated me from a number of images of God's absolute transcendence. God, the 'Unmoved Mover', the omnipotent, the immutable, the omniscient, but also God as the director of Creation, Fall and Redemption: all those images were shattered. It was not so much that I broke away from them; they just simply slipped out of my hands, as did the ecclesiastical and religious culture that built on these images in a modern or traditional way. This is what also happened to many of my contemporaries, friends and fellow students. Did the same thing happen to you? At least, it seemed to me, everyday life became devoid of these forms of transcendence. The void they left was filled with utopian conversations about a better life, with political critique and analysis, experiments with new forms of living and efforts to take responsibility for one's own life. The German philosopher Ernst Bloch typified this 'exodus from the house of the Father' as 'transcending without transcendence'. In his opinion, the issue no longer evolv-ed around God, but around *God's cause*: liberation, emancipation, and exodus, in short the Christian legacy. According to Bloch, the final and most definitive exodus that had to take place was the one from God himself: moving away from God, towards the kingdom of God. Faith in God had to be transformed into a faith in, or preferably a hope for the kingdom of God, which he regarded as a potential of the present that had not yet been realised. I could identify with that program.

Now that I am writing all of this down, it sounds so much more heroic than it actually was. For a long time, I kept trading on the shards of the old images of God, which I thought I had long discarded. Maybe, I was too inherently bashful to face the emptiness, or maybe I was too attached to the safety of those age-old forms, thoughts and structures. "A true exodus," the French Dominican and theologian Marie-Dominique Chenu wrote to me on several occasions, "requires the virtue of fearlessness." I am afraid that this is a virtue that I only possess to a very limited extent.

Trapped in the Transcendence of Everyday Life

This took place more than two decades ago. Life has changed rather dramatically since then, not just from a personal but also from a social and religious point of view. The concepts of God, holiness, and transcendence have very much fragmented. Furthermore, more than half of all social and cultural life in the Netherlands has become non-denominational or non-Christian. The desire to shape my personal life has since given way to hard and stubborn reality. Just think of the consequences of flexible working hours. What you have told me about constantly having to make arrangements for childcare appears to me an absolute nightmare as someone living on their own. Everyday life in all its aspects is constantly subject to review and the psychological stress that this brings is extremely high. Constantly having to establish and evaluate priorities in your life and work; needing to adapt your perspectives and self-image in the circles within which you move; to start again, whenever a period in your work or a relationship comes to an end, places a heavy strain on people's ability to cope with life and to hold on. It requires a great deal of courage and perseverance to repeatedly pick up the thread again. As a result of this, one could reach an impasse, become ill and lose the ability to work, which is what happened to me a couple of years ago. Suddenly you are confronted with the negative side of shaping your own life as a task that appears to be absolutely impossible. At its most basic level everyday life suddenly becomes a grey, suffocating blanket from which you cannot escape. It changes into an insuperable mountain, a 'transcendent' hurdle that simply cannot be endured. It is impossible to be the director of your own life when the key to the theatre is missing!

Whereas twenty years ago, as Bloch put it, one could still speak of 'transcending without transcendence'. In the current situation, exactly the opposite is true. There is only 'transcendence without transcending'. The paralysing odds of everyday life, after all, appear to make it impossible to take liberating, transgressing steps forward. How can you survive everyday life? I learned that the best way to do this, is to harness your courage and wait in hope until you find a key again, until cracks start to appear in this 'transcendence of the everyday' through which you can escape, which allows you to move on.

Everyday Life in Light of the Transcendent

In the meantime it might have become clear to you that I think the relationship between transcendence and everyday life is a rather complicated one or, in any case, one that has been a rather troublesome one during crucial periods in my life. First of all this troublesome relationship meant that I tried to free myself from some established forms of transcendence. On the one hand I have increasingly distanced myself from a number of old images of God that put everyday life in a straitjacket and have in any case become insignificant. I already mentioned some of these earlier. On the other hand I have learned that you are soon confronted with limits when you – separated from every external divine norm – want to take full control of your own life. The pursuit of autonomy may turn against you. When it does, life appears to be anything but constructable. Everyday life could even take on a form of transcendence more paralysing and oppressive than the transcendence of certain religious images of God. I find getting away from this ideal of constructability even more difficult than getting away from oppressing images of God.

Between the Scylla and the Charybdis of these forms of 'negative' transcendence, I went in search of a sustainable, stimulating, albeit only experimental relationship between everyday life and the transcendent. Where and how does transcendence appear in everyday life? For me, the transcendent appears as an opening in and as a depth dimension of everyday life, no matter how temporary, uncertain or hectic that life may be at times. Transcendence is present where light is shed on my existence and that of others – and that is something different from when I shed more light on my existence or that of others. Transcendence may also 'manifest' itself when things take a different course, or when, unannounced, someone or something presents itself as a different, better option.

Transcendence provides insight and broadens the horizon, but is only present for a moment, because it is almost as fleeting as life itself and sometimes even more so. It is similar to the light breaking through the clouds and the fleeting spot of light, which appears and skims the earth, followed by those very same clouds. This type of transcendence is not free from time and space, but has an interrupting effect by virtue of time and space. Furthermore, it is also not present without the clouds.

Transcendence is thus like a skimming light in a cloudy existence. As a flash of light it does not get rid of the shadows in life, but rather forms part of it by accentuating the contrasts. This light is a different, but specific aspect *of* everyday life, not something different *from* everyday life. To this extent it is immanent. At the same time, the light adds colour, significance, meaning and perspective to all that exists and places it within a horizon, something which the present cannot give itself; in that sense it is transcendent. It requires alertness to be prepared for this transcendence – precisely because of its fleeting nature. It requires attention and practice. In classical terms it also requires detachment and perseverance. The experiences I spoke of provided me with a great deal of wisdom about this. To some extent I have learned to rid myself of distorted, perpetuated, rigid images of the transcendent. I have also learned to patiently wait and see if something new, something important, something else comes along, even if this does not happen for quite a long time. These attitudes have become important to me. For that matter, their value has been emphasised in the various major spiritual traditions.

Now that I am writing this down, I realise that the contours of this transcendence are still fairly vague. I hope that I will be able to define them more closely through future letters in which I will reflect on specific experiences. For the moment, though, I would like to leave things as they are. I am very curious to hear about your experiences, and how the transcendent and everyday life are intertwined for you at the moment.

Yours,
Leo

Dear Leo,

Thank you for your letter. It sparked a chain of ideas, associations and questions in me, and also memories of how my own personal faith and thoughts have developed. You are right, there are very few theological topics quite as personal as God, the divine or the transcendent. In your letter it becomes very clear to me how much your images of those concepts or the stories you consider to be revealing, are intertwined with your biography and with those experiences that move you most deeply. To me writing and thinking about God, the divine or transcendence means painting a picture of how I see and would like to see myself and the world around me. It also involves thinking about questions such as the difference between sense and nonsense, good and evil, who or what I consult when I form a judgement and what authority inspires me when it comes to questions of meaning. This interpretation however of theology is the final stage (for the time being) of a long process of which I will describe only a few moments.

Back in Time

Your description of yourself as a sixteen-year-old made me wonder how I felt about God at that age. I recognised your story about the fresh breeze of secularisation as an experience that many people around me also shared. I had my own doubts as to whether or not the way I believed was in fact good enough, whether I lived sufficiently in line with my faith. This appears very strongly from the formula I wrote for my Confirmation in the Dutch Reformed Church as a nineteen-year-old in 1976.

> My faith in God plays an important role in my life. It gives meaning to my existence on earth and encourages me to make a contribution towards the realisation of His kingdom on earth. Since I tend to question my achievements in this respect – I more frequently fail than succeed – the knowledge that God will forgive me for all my failed attempts, helps me to constantly start again and not to become fatalistic or desperate.

When I look at that text now, I understand that I imagined the relationship between God and people as a relationship between an almighty God and a mere mortal. God passes judgement and forgives and I do my best, but am dependent on His forgiveness. The formulation that faith in God revolves around the Kingdom, reflects the spirit of the time. It is clear that I was influenced by both biblical theology and liberation theology, such as the student preachers in Wageningen, where I studied at the time. It emerged in their discussion groups, as well as in their sermons. The folder in which I keep the Confirmation formula also contains a list of activities and workshops you could join after Confirmation: thirty three in total. Many of these workshops became evident in the Sunday services through notices, stands and activities. I also took part in numerous campaigns, protests against the Atom Bomb, nuclear power and cruise missiles, and I went to women's peace camps. Later, I became active in the women's movement at the theology faculty in Utrecht and in the church; in women's reading circles; in committees and on boards and in the preparation of women's services.

    I have not even mentioned organising everyday life in such a way that it caused the minimum damage to the environment: no car, collecting paper and recycling it, separating waste, milk in bottles, never washing on Mondays in an effort not to contribute to the peak demand on the power supply – and these are just the things that became so much part of my daily routine that I still do them. However, there was also a time when I did my washing with soap flakes, used environmentally-friendly paint, only ate vegetables that were in season and so on. I did all this within the framework of God's kingdom on earth. Over the years I have lost that keen activism and when I look back at that time now, I am sometimes amazed at the amount of energy I had back then and ask myself what it was that possessed me. It most certainly was not just the spirit of the times or the group of people I hung out with – largely members of the Wageningen student group. Nor was it the unrestrained energy or the less constrained life of a student. It certainly had something to do with my image of God as well.

What you write about your 'activist' days – that it could be compared to 'an exodus from the house of the father', a 'farewell from God for the benefit of God's cause' – is also partly true for my faith in those days. For me there was no 'exodus from transcendence to everyday life', as you describe it. In my case, for a long time the concept of God remained synonymous with God's cause. What I thought God wanted from me or what belief in God was all about – working for Justice, Peace and the Wholeness of Creation – hung over me like a severe judgement. It was completely sufficient.

The phrase about 'the exodus of transcendence from everyday life' makes me wonder whether you should not in fact be speaking about the exodus of the Transcendent One from everyday life. The words 'transcendent' and 'transcendence' may look almost similar, but the difference in meaning is significant. After all, aren't you in fact describing the exodus of a transcendent God rather than the exodus of transcendence in its own right? After all, God's cause most definitely had transcendent dimensions. However, this transcendence was referred to differently – the cause was not immovable and immutable but still transcendent to everyday life and the individual person, because it provided a guiding ideal for the shape of everyday life.

For me, this raises the question whether it is because times have changed (and the fact that my way of life has changed quite dramatically) or because perceptions of who and where God is have changed, that you and I emphasize different aspects of our everyday way of life. Could it be that we and many other 'liberal' Christians are so much less active in public life or in the church, because there are no stories or representations that depict what it is that moves people and offers guidance for the discovery of the transcendent? It is just a question, not a statement. What I do know is that losing my faith in the transcendent God left a void, which not only had a liberating effect, but also introduced a 'crisis' to my life style.

The Iconoclasm of Feminist Theology

I have mainly lost faith in a transcendent and personal God through feminism and feminist theology. At Diedenoort, the advanced professional education course in facilitation management that I attended in Wageningen, I was attracted to the ideas of the women's movement after a project about domestic work. However, when I read Mary Daly's *Beyond God the Father,* as a theology student, the blinkers fell from my eyes. I cannot really explain why that book made such a big impression on me. It did not attach a name or meaning to experiences I had in the church or in theology, but reading the book nevertheless opened my eyes. Subsequently, it also led to new experiences – I saw and heard things in a different way, started to get more irritated about masculine language in the liturgy, about an interpretation that appeared to legitimise male domination. For example, in the way that psychologists of religion tried to defend the image of God as Father and in popular books about God as Father, I saw a defence and a legitimisation of male dominance and fatherly authority. Therefore, reading Mary Daly's book was quite an irreversible experience and it was impossible to return to the situation as it was before.

It had a major impact on my faith because the God I believed in or in whose name I had done so many things had become a problematic figure. Daly and other feminist theologians exposed the way in which that God was portrayed – Omnipotent, Omniscient, All-seeing, Creator, Father, King and so on – as so many interpretations of transcendence that were projections about male fantasies of power. I regarded the feminist theological criticism of the prevalent image of God in theology as revealing a tremendous iconoclasm. This meant that my criticism became more and more radical. Initially, I defended the idea that God transcended all images and that no image would suffice to represent God's greatness or mystery. This argument made it possible to find lost biblical and theological images of God and thus maintain a biblical, personal conception of God. But as I was further introduced into the theological and philosophical tradition, I felt an increasing urge to demolish rather than renovate. I increasingly started to see more clearly how the transcendence of God, expressed in images such as the 'immovable mover', or in qualities such as unchanging and immortal, was linked with a fear of or loathing of movement, change, transitoriness: concepts associated with the feminine. The female body became the symbol for the – horrific – reality to which the concepts of change and transitoriness referred. It became clear to me that representations of God's transcendence were rooted in a fear of the feminine and the female body in particular.

From Transcendence to Immanence, from God to the Divine

The feminist-theological criticism of the transcendence of God has led to a shift in the thinking about God and the divine. Many feminist theologians describe a God who is not transcendent to the world, but *immanent* in the world. This shift is also accompanied by a change in the way that people talk about God: from a metaphoric language in which God is represented as a person to a language in which God and the divine are no longer represented as a person or personally. Think of Mary Daly, who speaks of 'Being', when she talks about the divine. This double shift also occurs in the works of an influential theologian such as Carter Heyward. She refers to God as power-in-relationship and does not position God in heaven but rather among people.

I find this double shift from a transcendent towards an immanent and from a personal to an impersonal representation of God and the divine both exciting and challenging but for very different reasons. The most important reason lies in my desire for encounter, which shapes and gives meaning to living together, and in my desire for a source of life energy. To me, both feelings are related to what I mean by the divine. As I wrote at the beginning, thinking about the divine is related to what moves us deeply. Life energy lies at the roots of our being. Without life energy, shaping and giving meaning to living together diminishes. I also feel that it is a challenge to think about which words and expressions could be used to represent this immanent divine.

I have noticed that I am not consistent in my writings about God and the divine. Sometimes, I say that 'God is the source of life energy' but, on other occasions, I say that 'the divine is the source of life energy'. In the first case, life energy becomes one of the many aspects and qualities of God. It does not become clear that this image is the result of a break away from the image of the traditional, transcendent God. In the second case, I am expressing that I consider 'life energy' to be a quality 'of God'. I use it to denote a register, of concepts like the absolute, the ultimate, the sublime, the transcendent, the Holy. Perhaps the difference between those two expressions should be identified as the difference between a theistic and a non-theistic, an a-theistic representation of the transcendent. After all, the first form of expression appears to evoke a personal God whereas the second does not. Perhaps I should also see this moving back and forth between two forms of expression as an attachment to old forms and thoughts. I certainly found my own situation reflected in the things you wrote about this in your letter. However, I would like to add that I do not just simply move back and forth between old and new images of transcendence from attachment, but also because I am less attached and iconoclastic in my mind than I am in my emotions. I feel that this shows that those images and shapes are deeply rooted in the way I was brought up and in my relationships. A different time span and a different process are needed to change those images at the level of the emotions.

I notice that you hardly speak about God in your letter. Describing your more recent experiences of transcendence breaking through in your life, you opt for the image of light, and do not use the words God or the divine. This appears to be in contrast with the things you tell me about your motives for becoming a Dominican rather than a Buddhist. After all, at the beginning of your letter you formulated a number of very short questions that show what you believe to be the problems of the Buddhist position – a religion without images and representations. You also ask what to do about your own Christian tradition. I asked myself whether those were the questions that led you to the Dominicans. Are the questions you raised then still valid today, when old images of God no longer apply?

Let me return to the reasons for occupying myself with the relationship between immanence and transcendence. There is a further reason. I see it as a challenge to think about the difference between the divine and everyday things. I am particularly interested in whether the question or the statement that the divine can be found in everyday things also means that the divine coincides with these things. You deny this in the passage of your letter where you say that transcendence sheds its light on everyday life. You describe that existence as overshadowed or overcast. I would like to hear more about this. I find it hard to picture this image of the light that, on the one hand, is part of life and, on the other hand, adds a touch of colour to life, which life cannot add itself. I think your argument and your images contradict each other. While you keep transcendence and immanence closely together in your argument, you also create an image of tension between the two.

However, I am also convinced that the divine can be found in everyday things, but at the same time has to be distinguished from them. This finally brings me to the key question of how I could possibly make that distinction. What should I be paying attention to, what kind of qualities or senses should I learn to develop? For me, those questions are related to the way in which a person organises their day-to-day life. For example, when I say that the divine can be found in the encounter, this raises questions about the shape of that encounter. How can I enter into a relationship with someone, so that relationship can be the place where the divine is found? As far as I am concerned, this is about the shaping of everyday life. How can it be arranged in such a way that it offers openness, room or attentiveness to manifestations of the divine or transcendence? You write that preparedness for transcendence requires alertness, attention, practice, detachment and patience. In theory, I agree with you, but I often wearily ask myself why spiritual matters have to be so at odds with the worldly and hurried life of a working mother. Am I in fact looking for salvation for next to nothing? Possibly. Nevertheless, I think it is a realistic question for a way of life in which everyday life, with all its hustle and bustle and intensity, can be lived and experienced as the place in which the divine is found. That's all for now. I am curious to see what you have to say to this.

Yours,
Anne-Claire

Dear Anne-Claire,

I have had your letter about images of God, about immanence and transcendence, in front of me for some days now. It really made me think about what you write concerning your development, perception and ideas. The same applies to your questions about me. Ultimately, you are asking 'why do you think and feel the way you do?' It is hard to answer this question, let alone account for it. But your questions do help to clarify what it is I mean, and I hope I will successfully communicate this in our correspondence. Let me start with your last question, which, to a certain extent, summarises all your other questions and makes them more concrete: the one about the shape of everyday life in view of the transcendent.

Post-modern Transcendence: too Diffuse, too Close?

I share your difficulty about the shape of everyday life and the role of the divine in it. On the one hand, you describe how you went looking for an immanent God, for the immanent divine. Only such a God can be a source of 'life energy' in your everyday life. On the other hand, you establish that, as a result of the stubbornness of everyday life, there is very little evidence of divinity. Apparently it is hard to find a more intimate God. What you describe here is not only your own experience but also that of many others and mine. I think that this paradox is very closely related to the comments you made at the beginning of your letter. You ask whether the loss of transcendence from my everyday life did not in fact largely concern the loss of the transcendent God. Did not the transcendence of the ideal, the kingdom of God, politics, and the protests (with a certain religious shape!) remain? For a time they did but after a while these pointers began to falter. This is partly related to the political climate. But that's not all, as you quite rightly comment. My experience was that after the disappearance of the good old reliable God faith in a constructed social alternative ('kingdom of God') did not last very long. As far as that is concerned, I recognised myself very clearly in Friedrich Nietzsche's parable about the fool in the village square. The fool tells unsuspecting enlightened citizens that they have killed God without knowing it. The shockwaves of this enormous deed will engulf them and their faith in progress. The catastrophe already has indescribable dimensions. 'Who handed us the sponge to wipe out the entire horizon?', the fool asks, in a desperate attempt to characterise the prevailing culture after God's death. In retrospect, I must say that my own resorting to 'God's cause' was not much more than a temporary manoeuvre at the time of my religious alienation, as I suggested in my previous letter.

It is difficult to discover transcendence when there are no longer any clearly defined images of it in the form of a God, or a substitute ideal, a worldly image. When transcendence is not culturally embedded, it is 'nowhere' and 'everywhere', which almost comes down to the same thing. Such diffuse transcendence may be close but it is also intangible and almost impossible to define. You somehow feel its presence, but it does not really have an identity. I can imagine that someone would impatiently start looking for a shape to life that would make the religious, the transcendent, more clearly visible and easier to experience.

At the moment, I find it difficult to answer the question you raise about the shape of everyday life as a foundation for the divine. This is largely related to the fact that shapes in life, in everyday life, are temporary and, at the present moment anyway, subject to review. Everyday life is under constant review. I admit that this situation is one that is not without risk. It is not possible to maintain a shapeless life without a signifying framework that gives it meaning for some period of time. It is asking a lot to create these frameworks yourself. It is an impossible thing to do anyway because meaning is always something that is supra individual. From a social point of view, the fragmentation of meaning can lead to chaos, also in a person's personal life. One could get lost.

However, the existing situation also provides an opportunity to get rid of those images of transcendence one still carries around, even though they don't actually fit anymore. First of all, in this void we need to develop an attentive attitude: where does, no matter how diffuse, transcendence present itself in everyday life? Only when everyday life itself becomes the place in which transcendence can be found, will it subsequently be possible to attribute a more explicit place and shape to the transcendent within it as, for example, in a religious moment, a prayer, and meditation. Therefore, I think that the question with regard to the shape of everyday life and the divine, in brief, the question for a religious practice, can only be answered once one is open to the transcendent dimension of life.

Eckhart, or the Call to become like Martha

At several points in my life, when my images of transcendence and in particular of God faded or were shattered, I have consulted the medieval Dominican and mystic neoplatonic theologian Eckhart (1260-1327). Eckhart argues that people ultimately find their way to the hidden God. This God hides behind the God who manifests Himself: God as the Creator, as the Father, Son and Holy Spirit. These images refer to the 'created' God, the God who 'separated' himself from the hidden God, the 'non-created' God, in order to become the salvation of humankind. It is to this 'created' God that our human images of God refer. Eckhart states that the hidden God corresponds with being. 'Being is God'. Eckhart was accused of being a pantheist because of this, since he supposedly equates the divine with all things that are. In fact, Eckhart meant the following. There is a being that relates to concrete things, to the essence, the colour, the quantity of things: this is a chair with red velvet, like so many others. The being that refers to God is 'undivided': it is neither this nor that. 'God is not this or that'. 'God is nothing'. In fact, measured against the concrete reality, God is everything and nothing at the same time. The divine is incomparably different from every concrete thing or any concrete situation. God is transcendent. At the same time it is the foundation of things, the unfathomable dark, 'abysmal foundation' and in that sense, it is inherent to everything. Nothing can exist outside God. God is immanent.

According to Eckhart, if one wants to live towards God, one should try to live 'without why'. One should try to strip life of every 'in order to'. One generally performs an action with a particular goal in mind which, in turn, is aimed at an even remoter goal, and so on. Eckhart calls on us to put as much distance as possible from this type of instrumentalisation of activity. In fact, one should adhere to the action, the thing, the situation, the moment itself. The moment can then turn into an 'eternal now'. Eternity breaks through in the moment; it is the start of a time in which all moments in time are in a manner of speaking bunched together in 'undividedness'. This eternal now is no less than the 'breakthrough' of God.

Do we need to go into mystic seclusion for this? According to Eckhart, this is the last thing we should do. In a famous sermon on Luke 10:38-42, Eckhart fully supports Martha. Martha is grumbling at her sister Mary and is nagging Jesus to see if he cannot urge her to come and help serve the food instead of listening to his wonderful words. Jesus then says: 'Martha, Martha, you are worried and distracted by many things. There is need of only one thing. Mary has chosen the better part, which will not be taken away from her.' (Lk. 10:41-42). Eckhart's comment on this passage is astonishing. First of all, he says that Martha feels concern rather than anxiety. You are concerned when you are 'involved with' the things that have been entrusted to your care. You are concerned when you do your work in an uninterrupted and orderly fashion without being distracted or being caught up in it. You are anxious, however, when you are being caught up in or distracted by things. You then get engrossed 'in' things and are not 'involved with' things. Eckhart applies this distinction to Martha and Mary, and preaches the following:

> Now Christ says: 'you are concerned with many things' and not with the one thing. This means that when she stands upright on the circle of eternity, simple, pure and without actions, she is troubled by any form of 'means' which prevents her from remaining there in delight. Such a person is 'worried' by this, and is anxious and depressed. But Martha was securely established in mature virtue and had an unencumbered mind, free of any impediment. Accordingly she wished that her sister might be in the same state for she saw that she, her sister, was not yet *essentially* there. It was from the mature ground of her soul that she wished that her sister too should possess all that belongs to eternal blessedness. That is why Christ says: 'Only one thing is necessary'. But what is this one thing? It is God. This is what all creatures need, for if God took back what is his, all creatures would fall into nothingness. If God removed what is his from the Soul of Christ, where his spirit is united with the eternal Person, then Christ too would be no more than a creature. Therefore we have a great need of the one thing. Martha feared that her sister would remain trapped in her pleasant feelings and in the sweetness, and she wished that her sister might become as she herself was. Therefore Christ said: Be at peace, Martha. She 'has chosen the better part'. But this shall pass. The very highest thing that a creature can possess will be hers, and she will become blessed as you are blessed.

In other words, for Mary, contemplation competes with activity. Mary becomes totally engrossed in contemplation and, as a result, she remains trapped within herself. This makes her wonder if there is a chance that she might lose contemplation in her active life. She is 'engrossed in' contemplation, and not 'involved with' it. Mary is still in a preliminary stage of real religiosity, no matter how important that stage may be. One day she will become a Martha, and that is what we will all have to become. If we can be concerned and intimate with the reality that surrounds us, we no longer have to play contemplation and action off against each other. Eckhart is opposed to a dualist form of spirituality. Spirituality should be rooted in the concern for many everyday things. He is wary of exclusive religious practices anyway, like that of asceticism in religious life. All those practices profess to be just as many roads to God but they rarely are in fact.

Eckhart's sermons appeal to me, although I think they should be reinterpreted if their relevance is to be understood today. We could interpret Eckhart's 'being' as the 'meaning of life' in the sense of the world's being, and of you and me being in it. That meaning is transcendent. It simply exists. It does not coincide with every moment of our life, but constantly presents itself in it. We only have a limited grip on life; we have simply been 'thrown' into it, to quote the words of the German philosopher Martin Heidegger. We are only to a limited extent the creators of our meaning of life. According to Heidegger, the meaning of life reveals itself especially in our being intimate with a reality which is literally at hand. Just like Eckhart, he clearly distinguishes this attitude from instrumental and rational actions. Meaning breaks through when you are intimate with reality. This meaning is not created but simply described. It is not about a meaning that hovers outside or above things; no, it is about the meaning of things, about the meaning of your and my life. Your life and mine are lighted up, something lights up in it. This is what I meant in my previous letter with the image of a light breaking through. This does not mean that we should be satisfied with a passive openness. In fact, we need to have an active alertness for the meaning of our day-to-day actions.

Concerning the transcendence and immanence of meaning, in my opinion one does not exist without the other. They most clearly go together when you occasionally experience the ultimate meaning of what it is all about. Does my argument in favour of such openness and attention for the meaning of things come close to what you refer to as a source of energy for life? Or is there still not enough of a 'driving force' in it to keep you going from day-to-day in life?

Transcendence and Cultural Horizon

You wrote that by using the image of light I either intentionally or unintentionally increase the tension between transcendence and immanence. That is not what I am trying to do but nor do I deny that I want to maintain a distinction between the two. The reasons for this are related to another distinction and that is the one between two forms of transcendence. What do I mean by this?

I am thinking of the words of the sociologist Meerten ter Borg, concerning the transcendence of the symbolic universe or the cultural horizon. This horizon transcends individual experiences and also makes it possible to give a broader interpretation to them and communicate with others about them. Such a horizon gradually starts to become a small part of yourself, something immanent that you elaborate on, attach your own meaning to, and then pass it on to others. This is how tradition comes about. For a long time the Christian and ecclesiastical traditions formed such a horizon. The ties to this horizon are currently weakening and new horizons do not readily present themselves to address this ideological fragmentation. Is this a catastrophe? Have I lost all transcendence now? I have not, because it is another form of transcendence. It is the transcendence of the volatile intensity of light that cannot be easily forced into a horizon or into a (religious) frame of reference, which itself is in danger of overlooking that particular transcendence. This light is not available on demand and cannot be manipulated. It is unpredictable because it is something that just simply happens to you. It is precisely because of these characteristics that I want to distinguish the transcendent from the immanent. However, I explicitly add that it concerns the transcendent dimension of all our lives. I do not believe in anything transcendent that exists separately from our existence.

I have a question for you in connection with these two forms of transcendence. Sometimes it seems as though in your theology you equate transcendence with a new cultural horizon, a new feminine way of speaking. On several occasions you personify that horizon as a 'God-She'. At other times you seem to locate transcendence in what is taking place within the space created by that horizon, in the space between the self and the other, and in the encounter with the other, or, as I put it, the light that comes over us. I would like to believe that these two forms of transcendence are not separate from each other, but nevertheless, I want to emphasise the difference between the two. After all, I would think that light can also broaden or cut across that horizon, precisely at a time when even a new, seemingly liberating cultural horizon has once again become too narrow and is in need of renewal.

Let me put it another way. The transcendence for which I try to be receptive frequently presents itself in a period of silence. This silence precedes speaking and ultimately absorbs the speaking. Men and women are, as I often hear you say, irreducibly different by virtue of sexual differentiation. There are further irreducible differences in their way of speaking and in their cultural horizon. Let us just suppose that an equal relationship between men and women finally comes about. How can their irreducibly different ways of speaking be made mutually intelligible in that situation? Is there not a period of silence that makes this way of speaking audible and comprehensible every now and again and, at the same time, transcends and connects it, without equalizing them? Is this not what happens when men and women occasionally understand each other in wordless intimacy?

God and the Tone of our Conversation

Until now, I have been trying to avoid a crucial question you also seem to ask yourself. Does the perception of meaning mentioned above allow itself to be reconnected with images of God, more particularly, images of a personal God? And if so, how should we see this connection? This is how I see the question right now. When you relate perceptions of transcendent meaning to images of the divine this means that you are colouring those perceptions in more detail, that you are putting them in a framework, embedding them. From your letter I gather that you see such an approach as a-theistic, non-theistic, because God is not regarded as the source and origin of transcendent meaning, but 'merely' as a metaphoric intensification of it, a manner of speaking. For the time being though, I prefer not to label my position.

What many years ago made the Christian tradition more appealing to me than the Buddhist and to a certain extent even now, is the presence in Christianity of a 'transcendence with a human face' – in a God who makes himself known and is faithful in Jesus, who calls upon others to follow him. In other words, in a fellow man who invites you to become his neighbour. A face is less anonymous and less random than a ray of light in your existence. The relationship with the transcendent has had an ethical dimension in Christianity right from the very beginning. In the meantime, however, I also know that God's facial expression can all too easily become rigid and in time hold the faithful in a deadly grip. God's face has too often been a Medusa's head, which is best severed, just as Perseus did. Your iconoclasm – and that of many other women – against the tradition of patriarchal-transcendent images of God is an understandable and legitimate example of this beheading.

However, I am still intrigued by the significance of the human face in relation to transcendence. The revelation of meaning is something that falls to everyone but is always only partial. This is why we have to look for further enlightenment, which pre-eminently takes place when we face each other and engage in dialogue. What does talking to each other actually mean? For me at least it means the following: sharing our perspectives on the subject matter. The light that it sheds on the matter is very unusual and often very weak. However, in the process of passing it on and receiving it back, a new, bigger, stronger light emerges, a closer and more intensive enlightenment of meaning. The light that emerges in this way is much stronger than the individual contributions of the conversation partners. I think you say that this stronger light falls to us as mercy. A similar enlargement happens when you pay attention to the tone of a conversation. A conversation is more than the sum of two voices. It has a mutual tone that voices try to meet. This tone is like a third person joining the conversation.

Well then, the light of this enlightenment and the tone of the conversation may be linked to the image of a God as far as I am concerned. In this light, in this tone, God becomes visible, audible for just a moment to subsequently disappear into mystery once again. In my opinion such a representation of the divine can do justice to the volatile intensity of the experience of meaning many postmodern people have. Don't you agree? I look forward to your reply.

Yours, Leo

Hi Leo,

The relationship between images of God or the divine and Godself; the attitude to life of being involved with things in the here and now, through which we can find the transcendent in everyday life and transcendence with a human face as a characteristic of the Christian tradition are quite interesting issues raised in your letter. It took me some time to decide which issue to tackle first. I have decided to start with a reaction to your comments about the two different forms of transcendence, that is, the transcendence of the symbolic universe or the cultural horizon and the transcendence that goes beyond this cultural horizon or breaks it open at times when meaning is being manifest or presented and is not being made. You develop this theme in more detail on the basis of Meerten ter Borg's thoughts on the issue. You already touched upon that theme in your discussion of Eckhart's thoughts on a created God and a hidden God. I also begin with this issue, because you ask me how I see that relationship. You also find those two different interpretations of the concept of transcendence in my theology. On the one hand, you note that I argue in favour of a cultural horizon for women, condensed in my argument in favour of a God-She. On the other hand, I write that the divine manifests itself in the encounter with the Other.

Two Forms of Transcendence

I will use your explanation of Eckhart's ideas about transcendence as a basis for my reaction. You explain that Eckhart distinguishes between a 'created' God and an 'uncreated' God. He refers to the God who emerges from the images of God present in the culture as the 'created' God. Behind these the 'uncreated' God remains hidden. For Eckhart the latter God is 'transcendence' because He is everything and nothing. Paradoxically, this form of transcendence is radically immanent, because it is also the ground of being.

I see a parallel between the distinction that Eckhart makes between a 'created' and a 'uncreated' God and my ideas about the relationship between God-She and the divine or transcendent, which manifests itself in the encounters with others. This divine is probably the closest thing to what Eckhart calls the uncreated God. Personally, I would prefer to use the words infinite and inexhaustible for this form of transcendence, because I find it impossible to imagine the meaning of 'uncreated'. This infinite divine is transcendent, because it transcends the finite. It is the ground of being, because it is an infinite and inexhaustible source of life and constantly fosters new and different forms of being and living together. Furthermore, the transcendence of the divine is characterised by the fact that it cannot be represented exhaustively. The divine not only fosters life, the genesis, the movement and the change of life, but it also fosters and supports all cultural images of 'life' and of the divine.

Of course, these images are finite and restricted, or created, as Eckhart puts it. They are tied to time and place, because the in-finitely divine is found within the world of the here and now. I regard the expression God-She as a 'created' representation. It relates to a group of images of God that have one thing in common with the Dutch language. They all have the feminine gender. I am thinking of biblical images such as Wisdom, Spirit and similar to the images of nature such as earth, source and light. These are all 'feminine' words. If you use those words as an image for God, as an image of God, God becomes a 'she'.

Finite or 'created' representations of the 'infinite' divine are not devoid of transcendence. However, the transcendence of those images of God is of a different order than the transcendence of the infinite divine self. Those images form a horizon or a symbolic universe, which transcends the personal as with the general and universal. Furthermore, this universe is not just transcendent to the single individual, but also to any group of individuals. It provides them with a common story that unites them. Wherever the divine is an infinite, inexhaustible source of being, the representations of God form a finite, restricted representation of meaning.

In my opinion this transcending nature of the images of God becomes very clear in our first letters. We wrote about images that were transcendent to ourselves because they were prevalent in the society that we were part of, and because they were already there for us. To a large extent they determined our identity, including the way we speak and act, as well as our communication with others. The reason I go into so much detail about the transcendence of the horizon and the 'created' images of God is because I want to illustrate the role of transcendence. This horizon gives shape and direction to life, it forms our identity, legitimises our speaking and actions and mediates our exchanges – the verbal exchanges and the other gestures with which we enter into relationships. The function of that horizon – and therefore of the images of God – is of great political importance because, on the one hand, a cultural horizon is an expression of the dominant values in a social structure and, on the other, it also determines that social structure.

It is because of that political function that I attach so much importance to a horizon of and for women. I summarise this in my argument in favour of a God-She. To me, the point of all this is to have a collection of images that express which values and qualities give meaning to a woman's life or, from a woman's perceptive, contribute towards a good life for all. Without such representations, it is hard for women to tear away from definitions imposed on them by others. This is why women have to create images and tell stories with which they can surround themselves, with which they can shape their identity and their actions. Only then will they be able to shape their subjectivity and be able to communicate among themselves.

You are right, when you say that I locate transcendence partly in the horizon of and for women, in images of God that I bring together in the expression God-She. However, to be clear: this God-She does not have the qualities of the transcendent God of tradition. She is not immovable and unchangeable, but moveable and changeable. These qualities are related to the actual concept of an horizon itself. The horizon defines the space and the perception but also changes constantly, depending on the movement of the (collective) subject of that horizon, or depending on the course of this subject's life and the subject's search for meaning. However, the mobility of the horizon is also related to the tension between the finite character of the images of God and the infinite character of the divine. After all, images of God are never exhaustive; they are always inadequate when compared with the infinite divine. On the one hand, this explains the constantly renewed effort to give a name to that which transcends the existing names. On the other hand, it shows us that the images and names we use to depict the divine do not provide sufficient pointers in the search for the divine, but that one should be prepared for that which is unplanned.

Eckhart's Being Involved with Things

This takes me to the question as to how one could perceive or identify the diffuse manifestations of the divine. You used a sermon by Eckhart about Martha and Mary to illustrate your answer to this question. In this sermon he clearly shows, in your opinion, that an active and a contemplative life do not necessarily have to contradict each other. It is all about 'being involved with things'. But what does this 'being involved with things' mean? Eckhart explains it on the basis of the difference between 'concern' and 'anxiety'. If you are concerned, you are *involved with* things. If you are anxious, you are *engrossed in* things. If you are 'involved with' the things you are not being absorbed by those things; you do your work without becoming absorbed in the work. You are 'engrossed in' the things when those things or your work totally absorb you.

This explanation however does not really help me. I find it difficult to imagine this 'concern' in practice. I suspect that it is a practice in which the amount of attention with which the work is done, allows for openness for the 'unplanned' or 'unexpected' within everyday life. Nevertheless I am suspicious that 'not being absorbed by things' might imply a sort of inner distance in relation to the things that you are doing as a result of which your spirit is free to focus on other things. This suspicion arises as a result of Eckhart's formulation that 'she is saddened when she is hindered by something as if by a dividing mediation, which does not allow her the gratification of being above it'. He says this about Mary whom he refers to as being anxious, and being 'engrossed in' things. However, this appears to suggest that the one who is 'involved with' things, is 'concerned', and stands above things.

My problems with Eckhart's concept of 'concern' also stem from the fact that he introduces this concept in a sermon on Luke 10:38-42, in which the contrast between action and contemplation is a contrast between domestic work and study. As a result of this I associate concepts such as 'concern' and 'being involved with things' with domestic work. The main characteristic of this work is that it keeps recurring. It is, therefore, pre-eminently suitable for the inner distance or divided attention involved in being 'involved with things', that I referred to just now. You could argue that it is in fact a challenge to perform this work with attention and openness for the unplanned.

These reflections bring me to the question of whether Eckhart's 'concern' is not based on an inner division between body and soul. This question is reinforced even more by the fact that he regards the hidden God as 'being'. From your explanation it appears that Eckhart considers 'this being' as transcendent to that which can be perceived and recognised by the senses and consequently to matter. The consequence of this way of thinking about the transcendence of 'being' is that the hidden God cannot be recognised by the senses, but only by means of thought and reason. I have to confess that this latter aspect of Eckhart's ideas in particular made me think about the significance of his thoughts for our search for the transcendent in everyday life. Does this not mean that this transcendence, this hidden God, is primarily recognised and acknowledged via thought?

Don't get me wrong; I do not think that you are looking for the illumination of meaning of transcendence in everyday life in rational thinking only. Your passages about communication and involvement in which the senses play a key role, is evidence of that. However, I am curious to hear how you connect Eckhart's interpretation of the transcendence of being with 'awareness' or experience of transcendence in the communication with others.

Being is Sensory and Material

My question stems from my own – radically immanent – interpretation of 'being' as 'being involved with things'. I do not see 'being' as transcendent to the matter, but as rooted in the sensory, feeling and experienced matter. Colour, volume and rhythm are part of being, just as being is in-relation-to. Without this there is no meaning, but only death. Therefore, there is no being behind sensory, sensing and tangible matter; also, no transcendent, immaterial God in heaven, portrayed as pure or pure Reason, only the divine in the sensory, agile, relational matter. Because when 'being' is severed from its roots in living matter, which is something Western philosophers too often do, then the idea that 'being there', life on earth, starts in the womb, is forgotten. The French philosopher Luce Irigaray describes this denial of the roots in the womb in the following passage:

> The most wonderful, incredible, terrifying transfer goes [...] from the presence of the mother, in the mother, beyond the veil, to the presence of God, beyond heaven, beyond the horizon.

In this passage she wants to make clear that the transcendence of God is often a substitute for the transcendence of the motherly or for material life. The unmasking of this substitution calls for a renewed reflection on what philosophers and theologians understand by being, life, God and transcendence.

As already stated, I associate the divine with life. In doing so I conform to a certain extent to a prevailing theological tradition. One only has to think of the influential book by Dorothee Sölle's call to choose life in order to emphasise the divine as a source of life, inextricably bound up with the sensory, feeling and experienced matter. This material view of the divine as a source of energy of life has consequences for the knowledge of the divine. It implies that the perception of the divine surfaces via the senses, via the agile matter that has been put into motion. It makes it possible to say that the divine can be perceived in colour or smell, in space, in sound or in the intonation of a conversation, as you described in your last letter. As a result of this, the search for the divine is shifted from the interpretation of a tradition handed down, from the Word or the Bible as divine Revelation, to an interpretation of the perceptions of and in everyday life. An initial Revelation event confines the divine too much – the inexhaustible bubbling of things in life – and makes it impossible to perceive other, unexpected manifestations of the divine reality. Incidentally, this does not exclude the possibility that a word from the tradition about feeling and sensitive matter that moves our body is not relevant but it does exclude the possibility that the tradition is the only source of knowledge about the divine.

This radically immanent, material view of the divine determines my interpretation of 'being involved with things'. 'Being involved with things', in my opinion, calls for a high degree of sensibility, a refined sensory perception and a large degree of sensitivity in relation to other people and other things. When you write about openness and active alertness to the sense of our everyday life, I perceive this as the openness and attention of the senses for the impressions that the encounter with the other object and other human beings creates in us. I feel that this openly 'being involved with things' is a two-way process, outwardly and inwardly. It means touching and wanting to be touched by the other. I see the question of 'who are you' as being characteristic for the openness that you write about. That particular question is focused on the other person – invites the other person or the other thing to reveal who or what he, she or it is. But it is also focused on the person asking the question, that is, me, because I do not remain untouched by the encounter with the other. This touching of the ego may bring about a change in the fixed perceptions of who I am, what the world looks like, what the relationships with the other are and what is the meaning of life. The transcendent may manifest itself in this as the unplanned, the infinite divine, that disrupts and ruptures the finite, contrived perceptions.

With this, I think I have stirred up enough for one letter. I would still like to go into your passage about Christian tradition as the tradition of a 'transcendence with a human face', but I will leave this until next time. I look forward to hearing from you.

Yours,
Anne-Claire

Dear Anne-Claire,

It looks as though our explorations concerning the transcendent are moving in the same direction. At least, I can identify with the idea – that I would now like to put in my own words – that the divine is an inexhaustible source of life and light. That source constantly manifests itself in particular places but can never be identified with those places. The breakthrough of moments of grace in everyday life, for example, including encounters, through which life is given meaning and is concentrated into an 'eternal now' as it were, are the transcendence for which I long. I will return to this later, particularly in connection with the question as to why this experience hardly ever takes place. But first I would like to engage your questions and comments about Eckhart.

The Eternal Now as the Keeper of all Moments in our Life

I agree with you that the transcendence or the cultural horizon, as it gives shape to images of God, is an essential aspect of human society although it changes its own shape again and again. Images of God are contingent and constantly have to be sharpened and sometimes replaced. To a certain extent this is also Eckhart's view. He feels that we 'become devoid of God for the sake of God', and we constantly have to distance ourselves from imperfect images of God in order to get to the ultimate, the hidden God. This God is the eternally unchangeable. As a medieval, neoplatonic theologian, Eckhart inevitably thought this way. He did not think in terms of history. Consequently, you could indeed ask yourself whether Eckhart's attitude towards everyday life does not continue to be distant. Furthermore, what is the point of having such an eternal unchanging God behind all our images of God? I recognise your questions. Indeed, I feel that we can no longer think along the same lines as he did. Nevertheless, I will continue to be his interpreter and advocate for now, because I feel that his thoughts are still relevant today. I concentrate my defence on the notion of the 'eternal now'.

Eckhart made the prevailing neoplatonic theology of his time more dynamic. The one, that is unchanging, is not the focus for which one should be heading, but the abandonment of the many, the fickle and the inadequate. In a certain sense, there is no higher or lower. The 'eternal now' breaks through in time, in everyday life. That now 'encompasses all time', 'there is no before or after, everything is now'. Not a single moment is discarded. Such a breakthrough, let me say it in my own words this time, is the ultimate cumulative meaning of all moments of our life. We are in fact talking about a kind of storage here. All the moments of our life are treasuring up justice and given a place and a purpose and are protected from disappearing into forgetfulness. Eckhart's intense involvement in the unity between moments does not mean to say that he wants to stop them being separate but rather that he wants to see them develop into a unique relationship. He locates this involvement, which he believes everybody is potentially capable of having, in reason. However, this does not make Eckhart a rationalist in our ordinary sense of the word. His definition of reason is the human capacity to be open to all things and to their mutual relationship. Eckhart is much more concerned about intentionality, about a focus on and an openness to all reality that presents itself, and not so much about rationality in our meaning of the word.

The appeal of a spirituality in Eckhart's line is that – even though it stems from another time – it appears to provide an answer to the questions of today. God can never be grasped or objectified in images, dogmas or religious acts. God, the hidden, forms the relationship to the depth between all the moments of our life. When you look at it this way, you could even see Eckhart as a perfect guide for all those in search of a 'holistic' spirituality in their fragmented life. And it is for this reason that I do not conceal my sympathy for him. Nevertheless, he leaves me with one huge question. Why does the divine so very rarely break through in everyday life in a recognisable way? I would like to give this question some more thought and look for an answer.

Interruption and Remembering

We both see everyday life as the landing stage for the divine. That divine manifests itself in a way that is not defined and is ever changing. This is awkward, because in order to catch that divine, you sometimes have to develop an almost superhuman alertness with a very high degree of sensibility. No matter how difficult it is, you and I call for such sensibility and openness. All of this leaves me with a paradox, which I alluded to in my previous letter. How is it that in our (post)modern time the only remaining place where the divine can be found, everyday life, presents such barriers when it comes to finding God? Of all the places in which God can be found, should everyday life not be the one that is most easily accessible? Why do basic experiences constantly evade us and why are these experiences almost impossible to recognise? You raised this question in your first letter.

This question has been haunting me. In search of answers I read an article by Ugo Perone, the Italian philosopher and theologian, about the ambivalence of the transcendent in everyday life. It shed some light on this issue. His reflections enlarge on the thoughts of Walter Benjamin (1892-1940), the German philosopher and literature historian. Benjamin feels that in modernity everyday life is no longer founded within the context of a tradition with a story-telling history. It is becoming harder to interpret the events that happen. It is becoming increasingly difficult for these to become an experience, because, after all, experiences are linked to a tradition, a history of interpretation and a view of the world. Experiences are interpreted experiences. The consequence of this development is that experiences become like grains of sand, no longer embedded in an experience tradition. Everyday life loses its past and its future and becomes a momentary 'now' that transcends every earlier moment or even replaces and destroys it.

As the starting points for interpreted experience become rarer and more problematic, experiences increasingly become individual shocks, like ecstasy, a peak experience or a thrill. Such shocks manifest themselves most succinctly in the experience of happiness, satisfaction or fear. According to Benjamin, these shocks are so strong that their experience produces a defensive reaction in everyday life at the actual moment of experience itself. In the words of Perone they are 'so successful that this shock penetrates life and embeds itself in it in the form of a diffuse fear that is no longer dangerous'. Personally, I feel that this defensive reaction is related to the indefiniteness of the shock. It is not possible to immediately attach a specific meaning to it. After all, shock experiences are abundantly ambivalent; they can mean all sorts of things. This ambivalence is even more apparent when you no longer have a frame of reference to help you interpret these experiences.

Benjamin and Perone argue that (post)modernity is faced with the enormous task of finding a new entry to the shock experiences in our life – repressed and forgotten as they have become. In addition they will have to do without the old, trusted instruments of tradition, images of the world and frameworks of meaning. By way of a remedy for this problem Benjamin argues in favour of cultivating moments of interruption in everyday life. These are moments in which the sweeping flow of experiences is 'halted' or 'interrupted'. During that interruption a memory of the shock or experience will come back, the shock of happiness, enjoyment, pleasure or horror. Because in this memory the shock is rescued from oblivion and repression, Benjamin refers to these interruptions as 'redeeming moments'. The memory of the shocks as it were protects them and stops them from being lost to oblivion and repression. Benjamin locates instances of this type of interruption in everyday life among other things in boredom, waiting, contemplating, dreaming, gathering and in vacations. At all those moments, everyday life can once again be reminded of its original shock and in the process of remembering, meaning can be attached to it, a meaning which was not yet available at the time of the actual shock itself.

Perone indicates two consequences of this train of thought. First of all: in the interrupting memory the original shock is only presented in its weakened form; after all, it is not possible to entirely undo the smoothing effect of everyday life. It is only an echo. Secondly, and this is crucial: people only have access to the original shocks from their experiences via the interrupting memory afterwards, that is, indirectly. After all, at the actual moment the shock is both too intense and too repressed. The original shocks of our life, which Perone also describes in Eckhartian terms, as the abysmal basis of our life, are only stored and collected afterwards.

When I relate Eckhart's thoughts to those of Benjamin and Perone, I arrive at the following formulation. Occasionally an 'eternal now' breaks through in our everyday life. This light that breaks through, shines through all the moments of our life and brings them into a meaningful relationship. However, this breakthrough is forgotten and repressed before it penetrates full consciousness. That is why the moments, in which that 'external now' break through should in turn be collected, stored and made available in moments of an interrupting memory. We can think in terms of the way in which the unspeakable experience is unexpectedly found in words in a remembrance, a diary, a party, a celebration, a conversation.

I must admit that I can identify with this. Often, sudden changes I made in my life, came about after talking to other people. They would cause me to reflect on my memories and see my situation in a new light. Those memories often appeared to have been forgotten or dormant. In conversations, I became aware of them once again, usually much later. They could then still return from the forgotten origin into the mobilising force of changes that confronted me.

The Never Ending Search for the Shape of Life

If this line of thought is convincing, then my argument in favour of an openness to the 'eternal now' and yours in favour of the sensory, sensible encounter with others, becomes somewhat precarious. Are our arguments still tenable in the way in which we presented them? Isn't this really just about experiences that are too stark, too strong and, as a result, almost immediately disappear, are covered up or repressed? And does this not pre-eminently apply to the sense of touch, which Irigaray refers to as the mother of all senses? She says that touching – and I think quite rightly so – is about something that cannot be preserved and cannot be represented. You will probably say: yes, that is why, in addition to the transcendence of the 'event' and of the experience, I am now looking for that other form of transcendence, the one of words, the cultural horizon, the images of God, in short, the form of transcendence that offers a framework for communication and for the continuation of mutual understanding. But if it turns out to be the case that the chances of such a horizon are currently very small, even though absolutely necessary, what happens then?

Do the remedies of Benjamin and Perone offer any greater comfort? Should we restrict ourselves to an exercise in standing still, looking back and remembering for the time being because there is no real common horizon? Should we not try to gain access to (sensory) original experiences in a filtered way, as these present themselves in touches, encounters, sensations of fear and enjoyment? In fact, I think that this could be an appropriate way in our (post)modern condition. I am very tempted to review our established liturgy in an effort to put this insight into a concrete form. Should we not consider liturgy as a feast that is, as it were, the organised interruption of everyday life? Could the Eucharist as a memory of the life, death and resurrection of Christ not offer a special possibility to suddenly remind you when and in what respect life was hell or in fact a resurrection for you?

However, at other times it seems to me that such a review of the ecclesiastical celebration of the community is just a little bit too easy. Are the ecclesiastical celebrations not characterised by a religious conceptual universe that has become impossible to understand or been put under too much pressure? Should we not simply file away the liturgies forever and convert the remaining churches and chapels into 'story-telling houses', in which people recall those things that touched them most deeply of all? When I feel as though I am an iconoclast – which I sometimes do – I think that this is indeed the direction in which we should be heading. The stories told in these houses could be linked to elements of Christian and also other (religious) traditions – depending on the storyteller's background. From the beginning, some frame of reference would have to play a role in this, even if it were only because not a single memory can be organised without some basic frame of reference. Regardless of the way it comes in, I feel that it is vitally important for people to be given access to the transcendent dimension in their everyday life in this kind of way. People have to be given the opportunity to practice making themselves aware of this dimension and attaching words to it. To me this appears to be of vital importance for everyone's mental health, particularly in a situation in which the cultural horizon has fragmented and for the time being will continue fragmented.

You will notice that the question you ask in your first letter about the shape of everyday life and the place that the transcendent and religion has in everyday life, has stuck in my mind. The importance of that question became clearer to me only in the course of our exchange of letters, in particular the reflection on remembering and interruption. I have to reconsider the comment I made in my last letter about everyday life being the place in which transcendence is found and that this transcendence should be given a place and a more explicit shape along the way. It is not possible to perceive the transcendent without shape. Without observing moments of interruption and without remembrance, we do not have access to what we perceive and experience. On the other hand, if we have not perceived anything, we cannot remember it either. Shapes are a vital mediation, in particular when it concerns something that is as intangible as transcendence. There is no shapeless access to transcendence. However, you will notice that I am still looking for what this shape should look like. For the time being I have no well-defined representations of it. At the very most a remote inkling of the direction in which I should be looking. I look forward to hearing from you.

Yours,
Leo

Dear Leo,

Your last letter gave me quite a lot to think about. On the one hand, I was touched by the idea that the way of remembering is essential in the interpretation of experiences of transcendence. I saw an answer to the question about the shape of life in (collective) remembering and reflecting on the meaning of certain experiences. Furthermore, I felt that this also offered possibilities for the process of giving shape to a shared horizon. However, I was surprised and even a little shocked by the idea that transcendence involves such an intrusion in everyday life that it is repressed. I wondered whether I had perhaps missed something in your letters. My surprise made me think about the things we have exchanged. It prompted me to re-read your letters and to review what each of us had written about transcendence.

When I re-read the letters, I noticed that we feel the same about many things. We both see everyday life – in particular the communication with the other – as a place in which to find the divine. However, I also noticed differences, particularly in our interpretation of the concept of transcendence. You use an ambiguous concept of transcendence, while I am tempted to see the transcendent and the divine as an extension of each other. This is what I discovered in my efforts to understand exactly what you mean by the idea that the experience of transcendence involves a shock that initially was repressed. Before I go into this line of thought in more detail, I would like to return to the idea that communication with the other is the place in which transcendence is found.

The Encounter with the Other: the Place in which Transcendence is found

We both write that the encounter with the other is the place in which the transcendent can be found. That thought also encompasses our ties with the Christian tradition. You express that connection in your answer to my question about why at a certain time you became a Dominican and not a Buddhist. You wrote that the appealing thing about the Christian tradition is 'the presence of a transcendence with a human face, in a God who makes himself known, and who is faithful. [...] A face less anonymous, less random than a ray of light in your life. In Christianity the relationship to transcendence has had an ethical dimension right from the very beginning.' I recognise an important aspect of my own solidarity with Christian tradition in your words. In particular, the expression 'transcendence with a human face' reflects my own fascination for the concept of the incarnation; a concept with which I establish and continue to maintain the link with Christian tradition.

I have now been thinking and writing about the significance of God's incarnation for the relationship between God and humankind for many years, particularly for the relationship between God and women. My thoughts on this have developed over the years. At first, I was fascinated by Emmanuel Levinas' idea that a trace of the divine Other can be found in the face of the other person. In your words, I hear echoes of Levinas' thinking, particularly in your preference for terms like 'the face of the other'. For me, Levinas opened up the possibility to consider the incarnation of God in women. His ideas implied that the divine Other, the Transcendent, manifests itself in the face of another person of the female sex. This thought opened up numerous prospects. It became possible to show that no attention was paid to the face of women in the relationships between men and women. It made it possible to imagine a recognition and acknowledgement of the authority of (the face of) women and as a result of this of her subjectivity because her face could not represent a trace of the divine Other. Finally it opened up the possibility to think of the divine Other as a Transcendent in the feminine, an Other-She. When I lost my faith in God the Father, the personified God of the fathers and of the philosophers – and as a result of this in a transcendent Other – the need to see women as a personification of a transcendent God disappeared.

This loss also had consequences for my thinking about the communication with the other as a place where the divine could be found. Initially, I saw the communication with the other as an encounter in which the transcendent Other manifested itself in the face of the other person. Now, I think that this other person him or herself is the transcendent because he or she is irreducibly different from me. This shift results in the encounter no longer being the place in which transcendence is found, because I meet the Transcendent in or via the other, and the transcendent manifests itself in the space between the ego and the other. This interspace is created when the difference, the transcendence of the other, is not removed but protected. This respect prevents a situation in which the vision of one of two subjects is wiped out and that what was meant to be a dialogue is reduced to a monologue. Transcendence manifests itself in this interspace as a 'third party' who transcends the subjects of the encounter, as the change that occurs in the thoughts of the subjects as a result of the dialogue or as the fibre of meaning that they both weave in their mutual communication. However, I do not see the interspace purely as a place in which transcendence is found, but also as a place in which the divine is found. In this interspace, the 'source of energy of life' manifests itself as a third party that belongs to neither one nor the other, but which both share.

I thought that you were thinking along similar lines with respect to the communication with the other as a place in which transcendence can be found. This idea came to me as a result of your passages about the development of a more intense light, when each party contributes his or her light, and a sentence such as 'God becomes visible and audible for a moment and subsequently disappears into mystery once again.' This is why I was taken aback by your explanation of the perception of transcendence as a shock that is repressed and forgotten. It shocked me into recognising the difference between us. It was a shock of incomprehension and defence. I have found it hard to relate this experience to our explanations of the communication with the other being a place in which transcendence can be found. Does the communication with the other bring about such an experience of shock? What kind of communication is this then, and what kind of interpretation of transcendence are we talking about here? These questions and reactions are very much related to my own thoughts on the relationship between everyday life and the transcendent.

The Flesh: Landing Stage for the Transcendent

My interpretation of everyday life means that I have to disagree with your vision of everyday life as the landing stage for the transcendent which, paradoxically and at the same time, places a barrier to finding the divine and God. This difference also arises from a different view of the transcendent and of transcendence. Let me start with the first point. In my view, everyday life and the material, the flesh, are extensions of each other. The flesh, that feeling, sensitive and sensory matter, is the precondition for 'Dasein', to use one of Heidegger's terms. The thought that the being of things is rooted in matter implies that we only have access to ourselves and the world around us via the flesh or feeling and sensitive matter. I already wrote to you that this meant that the flesh has a dual orientation – outwardly and inwardly. This dual orientation is most clearly expressed in terms of touching. When it comes to touching the other person or the other thing, it is hard to make the distinction between (active) touching and (passive) touching. While touching I am being touched, this is how subtle the exchange of sensations and the movement between inside and outside is. The things that apply to touching also apply for the sensations of the other senses, because these are also rooted in vibrating, agile matter. This means that during perception – seeing, hearing, smelling, tasting and feeling – the flesh points outwardly, opens itself up to the other, to the world. This openness is however also an openness to touch, to being touched, to being moved or becoming ecstatic.

When I relate my thoughts about the flesh to the transcendent, I see first of all the perception of the transcendent as a perception of the flesh, as being touched in a sensory way. I think of my heart missing a beat, of my muscles tensing up when the story of the other person touches me, of intensified breathing in nature, of the physical arousal that you experience when everything falls into place when you are singing or writing something. There are experiences that give me the strength and energy, give me joy in life and provide insight into the way in which I see myself, the world and the divine. They shed light on the values that I live by or would like to live by, on the difference between good and evil. This is why I refer to them as experiences of transcendence.

This is a name I attached to them afterwards, but that does not alter the fact that these experiences are primarily movements in and of the flesh. This movement of the flesh forms the basis of a chain of subtle transformations, in which sensory perceptions are translated into images and representations. I imagine this process of transformation as a movement back and forth from inside to outside - between the sensory matter of the flesh and the world of representation. This transformation process is made up of several stages. It goes from the sensory perception to the (sub-conscious) depiction of the body, where needs, desires and cultural factors meet. The next stage goes from the subconscious depiction of the body to the image via the imagination. The imagination forms the link between the subconscious and the conscious, in short, between flesh and word. In my representation of the divine as a source of energy of life, I try to express the following thought: the image is rooted in the flesh.

Against this background – which presupposes a great deal of continuity between the sensory perception and the image of the transcendent and the divine – I have some problems with your idea that the perception of transcendence is a shock perception and an invasion of everyday life. For me both words are associated with violence. I therefore find it hard to associate these words with our lyric descriptions of the communication with others. If this communication gives rise to this type of communication, what is the relationship between individual encounters? Is the repression of sensory experience not a typical reaction of a victim of sexual violence? And what kind of interpretation is given to the concept of transcendence that is associated with shock and invasion? To be honest with you, those words make me think of old representations of experiences of transcendence, in which God gains access to a person's heart by force.

Experiences of Transcendence as Ambiguous Experiences

It was only after I realised that for you the shock of the invasion of everyday life was caused by the fact that it is an ambiguous experience or an experience with a surplus of meaning that I was able to accept the idea and to reflect on what I thought of it. This reflection raised two points. First, it made me aware of the fact that I see the transcendent and the divine as synonymous, which I also associate with good things, the power in relationships, or with energy of life. I again realised that I cannot describe experiences of physical suffering, finiteness, breaks and iconoclastic criticisms as experiences of the divine. The shock experience you write about does make it possible to describe both types of experience as experiences of transcendence because you give a different and perhaps more literal meaning to the word transcendence. It is about experiences that transcend the categories of everyday life; experiences that are bigger, heavier, appearing to be more intensive than the concepts that are used to give meaning to everyday life, or that are more ambiguous because violence and pleasure, ecstasy and the overstepping of limits go hand in hand. This thought strongly reminded me of the point that Sharon Welch put forward in her latest book, which is that the perception of transcendence is an essential part of the continued work towards justice but is also fundamentally amoral. She says this in a passage about the ecstasy that can be evoked in a group process, in collectively working towards a goal. She describes it as an experience to be part of powers that are greater than the individual. She says that this type of perception of transcendence is fundamentally amoral because both conservative and liberation movements have this ecstasy. She draws the conclusion that this perception is no foundation for the truth or tenability of an ethical statement. This idea made me think about my definition of the transcendent as a source of energy of life. Welch points out that the transcendent can be both a negative and positive force; one that can heal and that can destroy. To some extent this also applies to the energy of life, because it is a force that can break through set forms, associations or traditions. In that case the perception of transcendence is a mixed experience of pain and liberation, which only gradually – in the process of remembering, reflecting and talking about things with others – is given meaning, which is something you have said as well.

I already told you at the beginning of this letter that your argument in favour of remembering and of shaping everyday life, which means that there are moments and ways of remembering, appealed to me very much. It is an idea in which the everyday practice of telling and interpreting the things that happen to you is given meaning. As a result of the process of remembering, the experiences are given value and direction, I see this reflecting and remembering as a part of creating a horizon; of a web of stories that interprets the experiences and subsequently also produces them. This is at least how I interpret the end of your letter, in which you note that perception and imagination go hand in hand with transcendence. With this you give an initial answer to the question of how everyday life can be shaped so that it can be a place in which the transcendent can be found.

I like the wording of the interruptions to remember as 'redeeming moments'. However, and I think this signifies another difference between us, I would not only want to associate those moments with the memory of the big shocks in our lives, but also with the little moments in our lives: an encounter, a touch that was so fleeting, so much in passing that its true meaning was not understood at the very moment itself; that was not perceived as the encounter that radiated energy, as the touch that caused a subtle shift in perspective. This brings me back to my question about the shape of life that I raised in my first letter without knowing how that should give shape to my everyday life. Instances of active remembering could become instants of the saving moment in favour of perceptions of the divine in everyday life. After all, when the transcendent manifests itself in everyday communication with the other, don't you still need moments when the day is regurgitated and the encounters are remembered so that the unexpected is not lost?

Yours,
Anne-Claire

References

E. **Bloch**, *Atheismus im Christentum. Zur Religion des Exodus und des Reichs*, Frankfurt a.Main 1968.
M. **ter Borg**, *Een uitgewaaierde eeuwigheid. Het menselijk tekort in de moderne cultuur*, Baarn 1991.
J. D. **Caputo**, *The Mystical Element in Heidegger's Thought*, Fordham ³1990.
T. **Chanter**, *Ethics of Eros. Irigaray's Rewritings of the Philosophers*, New York/London 1995.
M. **Daly**, *Beyond God the Father. Toward a Philosophy of Women's Liberation*, Boston 1973.
G. **Dekker** a.o., *God in Nederland 1966-1996*, Amsterdam 1997.
L. **Dupré**, *The Other Dimension. A Search for the Meaning of Religious Attitudes*, New York 1972.
I.C. **Heyward**, *The Redemption of God. A Theology of Mutual Relation*, Lanham 1982.
L. **Irigaray**, *L'éthique de la différence sexuelle*, Paris 1984.
L. **Irigaray**, *J'aime à toi. Esquisse d'une félicité dans l'histoire*, Paris 1992.
G. **Jantzen**, *Power, Gender and Christian Mysticism*, Cambridge 1995.
G. **Mak**, *Hoe God uit Jorwerd verdween*, Amsterdam/Antwerpen 1996.
Meister Eckhart, *Selected Writings*, [translation O. Davies], London 1994.
A.-C. **Mulder**, 'Het bouwwerk God de vader: niet renoveren maar slopen', in: P. de Vries e.a. (eds), *Aan het hoofd van de tafel: feministische artikelen over vaderlijk gezag*, Amsterdam 1988, 100-115.
A.-C. **Mulder**, 'Doorzichtige weefsels, beweeglijke ruimten', in: *Ophef. Tijdschrift voor hartstochtelijke theologie*, 4 (1997) 4, 25-29.
A.-C. **Mulder**, M. **Kalsky**, 'Verschillen als uitdaging. Een briefwisseling over ruimte voor vrouwen', in: M. Kalsky e.a. (eds), *Bouwen met los zand. Theologische reflecties op verschil en verbondenheid*, Nijmegen/Zoetermeer 1997, 87-122.
A.-C. **Mulder**, *Divine Flesh, Embodied Word. Incarnation as a Hermeneutical Key to a Feminist Theologian's Reading of Luce Irigaray's Work*, Utrecht 2000
U. **Perone**, 'Die Zweideutigkeit des Alltags', in: B. Casper, W. Sparn (eds), *Alltag und Transzendenz. Studien zur religiösen Erfahrung in der gegenwärtigen Gesellschaft*, Freiburg/München 1992, 241- 263.
S. **Sikka**, *Forms of Transcendence. Heidegger and Medieval Mystical Theology*, New York 1997.
W. **Derkse** a.o., *Subliem niemandsland. Opstellen over metafysica, intersubjectiviteit en transcendentie*, Best 1996.
D. **Sölle**, *Wählt das Leben*, Stuttgart 1980.
N. **Thera**, *The Heart of Buddhist Meditation*, London ²1969 (1962).
D. **Turner**, *The Darkness of God. Negativity in Christian Mysticism*, Cambridge ²1996 (1995).
S. **Welch**, *Sweet Dreams in America: Making Ethics and Spirituality Work*, New York 1999.

List of Contributors

Dr. Erik Borgman (Amsterdam 1957) is a lay Dominican. He studied theology and philosophy at Nijmegen University where he lectured from 1984 till 1989. In 1983 he was Fulbright Scholar in Residence at Mercyhurst College in Erie, Pennsylvania. In 1990 the Dutch Dominicans commissioned him to write a theological biography of Edward Schillebeeckx. He published: *Edward Schillebeeckx; a Theologian in his History. I: A Catholic Theology of Culture (1914-1965)* (London 2002). At present, he is the director of the Heyendaal Institute for the interdisciplinary study of theology, science and culture at Radboud University Nijmegen.

Dr. Stephan van Erp (Tilburg 1966) studied philosophy at Nijmegen University and theology at the universities of Tilburg and Oxford. He was a researcher of the Dominican Study Centre for Theology and Society in Nijmegen from 2000 to 2003. In 2004 he published *The Art of Theology. Hans Urs von Balthasar's Theological Aesthetics and the Foundations of Faith* (Leuven 2004). Currently he is the research coordinator of the department for Theology and Medical Sciences of the Heyendaal Institute for the interdisciplinary study of theology, science and culture at Radboud University Nijmegen. He lectures dogmatic theology at the Theological Faculty of Tilburg.

Dr. Manuela Kalsky (Salzgitter Bad 1961) is director of the Dominican Study Centre for Theology and Society in Nijmegen. She received her PhD at Amsterdam with her thesis on the different views of women in their cultures on Christ. She published *Christaphanies. Die Re-Vision der Christologie aus der Sicht von Frauen in unterschiedlichen Kulturen* (Gütersloh 2000).

Dr. André Lascaris (Amsterdam 1939) is a Dominican. He received his PhD at Oxford University and lectured in Pretoria (SA), Nijmegen and Amsterdam. He fulfilled several administrative functions in his Order, was involved in peace work for Northern Ireland and published numerous articles and books on conflict, violence, forgiveness and reconciliation. He has been a member of the staff of the Dominican Study Centre for Theology and Society since its foundation in 1988.

Dr. Anne-Claire Mulder (The Hague 1956) studied housekeeping economics at Wageningen University and theology at Utrecht University where she received her PhD with her book *Divine Flesh, Embodied Word. Incarnation as a hermeneutical key to a feminist theologian's reading of Luce Irigaray's work*, Utrecht 2000. She worked as a research fellow at the Dominican Study Centre for Theology and Society from 1994 to 1998. At present she lectures in feminist theology at Kampen University.

Leo Oosterveen (Zeist 1954) is a Dominican and regent of studies of the Dutch Dominican Province. He holds master degrees in theology and philosophy at Nijmegen University. He is a member of the staff of the Dominican Study Centre for Theology and Society since its foundation in 1988.

Dr. Robert J. Schreiter (USA, 1947) is Vatican Council II Professor of Theology at the Catholic Theological Union in Chicago, and Professor of Theology and Culture at the Radboud University in Nijmegen. Among his many books are *Constructing Local Theologies* (1985) and *The New Catholicity: Theology between the Global and the Local* (1998).

Dr. Ad Willems (Rotterdam 1926) is a Dominican. He studied in Basel, Strasbourg and Münster where he received his Ph.D. He is an emeritus professor of Nijmegen University where he lectured systematic theology. He published on ecclesiology and the history of soteriology, on Karl Barth and Friedrich Schleiermacher. He was a member of the staff of the Dominican Study Centre for Theology and Society between 1988 and 1997.

Dominican Study Centre for Theology and Society (DSTS)

Address:
Erasmusgebouw
P.O. Box 9103
6500 HD Nijmegen
The Netherlands
e-mail: *dsts@dsts.nl*
website: *www.dsts.nl*

Religion – Geschichte – Gesellschaft
Fundamentaltheologische Studien
hrsg. von
Johann Baptist Metz (Münster / Wien),
Johann Reikerstorfer (Wien)
und Jürgen Werbick (Münster)

Jürgen Manemann;
Johann Baptist Metz (Hg.)
Christologie nach Auschwitz
Stellungnahmen im Anschluß an Thesen von Tiemo Rainer Peters
Bd. 12, 2. Aufl. 2001, 192 S., 15,90 €, br.,
ISBN 3-8258-3979-6

Angela Büchel Sladkovic
Warten auf Gott – Simone Weil zwischen Rationalismus, Politik und Mystik
Bd. 15, 2004, 352 S., 24,90 €, br.,
ISBN 3-8258-6912-1

Barbara Nichtweiß (Hg.)
Vom Ende der Zeit
Geschichtstheologie und Eschatologie bei Erik Peterson. Symposium Mainz 2000. Mit Beiträgen von Klaus Berger, Ferdinand Hahn, Karl Lehmann, Eduard Lohse, Hans Maier, Christoph Markschies u. a.
Bd. 16, 2001, 344 S., 25,90 €, gb.,
ISBN 3-8258-4926-0

Maureen Junker-Kenny; Peter Kenny (eds.)
Memory, Narrativity, Self and the Challenge to Think God
The Reception within Theology of the Recent Work of Paul Ricœur
Bd. 17, 2004, 232 S., 20,90 €, br.,
ISBN 3-8258-4930-9

Benjamin Taubald
Anamnetische Vernunft
Untersuchungen zu einem Begriff der neuen Politischen Theologie
Bd. 18, 2001, 208 S., 20,90 €, br.,
ISBN 3-8258-5151-6

Detlef Schneider-Stengel
Christentum und Postmoderne
Zu einer Neubewertung von Theologie und Metaphysik
Bd. 19, 2002, 328 S., 25,90 €, br.,
ISBN 3-8258-5011-0

Jürgen Werbick
Gebetsglaube und Gotteszweifel
Bd. 20, erweiterte 2. Aufl. 2005, 296 S., 20,90 €, gb., ISBN 3-8258-5379-9

Paulus Budi Kleden
Christologie in Fragmenten
Die Rede von Jesus Christus im Spannungsfeld von Hoffnungs- und Leidensgeschichte bei Johann Baptist Metz
Bd. 21, 2001, 448 S., 40,90 €, br.,
ISBN 3-8258-5198-2

Bernhard Nitsche
Göttliche Universalität in konkreter Geschichte
Eine transzendental-geschichtlichen Vergewisserung der Christologie in Auseinandersetzung mit Richard Schaeffler und Karl Rahner
Bd. 22, 2001, 562 S., 40,90 €, gb.,
ISBN 3-8258-5136-2

K. Hannah Holtschneider
German Protestants Remember the Holocaust
Theology and the Construction of Collective Memory
Bd. 24, 2001, 232 S., 25,90 €, br.,
ISBN 3-8258-5539-2

Ulrich Willers (Hg.)
Theodizee im Zeichen des Dionysos
Nietzsches Fragen jenseits von Moral und Religion
Bd. 25, 2003, 248 S., 20,90 €, br.,
ISBN 3-8258-5561-9

LIT Verlag Münster – Berlin – Hamburg – London – Wien
Grevener Str./Fresnostr. 2 48159 Münster
Tel.: 0251 – 62 032 22 – Fax: 0251 – 23 19 72
e-Mail: vertrieb@lit-verlag.de – http://www.lit-verlag.de

Ansgar Koschel (Hg.)
Katholische Kirche und Judentum im 20. Jahrhundert
Mit Beiträgen von Herbert Bettelheim, Ernst-Ludwig Ehrlich, Gabriel Padon, Gerhard Riegner, Herbert Smolinsky und Erich Zenger
Bd. 26, 2002, 176 S., 17,90 €, br.,
ISBN 3-8258-5507-4

Lydia Bendel-Maidl
Tradition und Innovation
Zur Dialektik von historischer und systematischer Perspektive in der Theologie. Am Beispiel von Transformationen in der Rezeption des Thomas von Aquin im 20. Jahrhundert
Bd. 27, 2004, 608 S., 45,90 €, br.,
ISBN 3-8258-5589-9

Christian Heller
John Hicks Projekt einer religiösen Interpretation der Religionen
Darstellung und Analyse – Diskussion – Rezeption
Bd. 28, 2001, 528 S., 40,90 €, br.,
ISBN 3-8258-5528-7

Peter Zeillinger
Nachträgliches Denken
Skizze eines philosophisch-theologischen Aufbruchs im Ausgang von Jacques Derrida. Mit einer genealogischen Bibliographie der Werke von Jacques Derrida
Bd. 29, 2002, 296 S., 35,90 €, gb.,
ISBN 3-8258-6144-9

Kurt Appel
Entsprechung im Wider-Spruch
Eine Auseinandersetzung mit der politischen Theologie des jungen Hegel
Bd. 31, 2003, 208 S., 29,90 €, br.,
ISBN 3-8258-6605-x

Bertil Langenohl;
Christian Große-Rüschkamp (Hg.)
Wozu Theologie?
Anstiftungen aus der praktischen Fundamentaltheologie von Tiemo Rainer Peters. Mit Beiträgen von U. Engel, J. Manemann, J. B. Metz, O. H. Pesch, H. Steinkamp u. a.
Bd. 32, 2005, 328 S., 24,90 €, br.,
ISBN 3-8258-8119-9

Nicoletta Capozza
Im Namen der Treue zur Erde
Versuch eines Vergleichs zwischen Bonhoeffers und Nietzsches Denken
Bd. 33, 2003, 336 S., 29,90 €, br.,
ISBN 3-8258-6667-x

Peter Hardt
Genealogie der Gnade
Eine theologische Untersuchung zur Methode Michel Foucaults
Bd. 34, 2005, 408 S., 34,90 €, br.,
ISBN 3-8258-8484-8

Ernst-Wolfgang Böckenförde
Kirche und christlicher Glaube in den Herausforderungen der Zeit
Beiträge zur politisch-theologischen Verfassungsgeschichte 1957 – 2002
Bd. 36, 2004, 456 S., 39,90 €, gb.,
ISBN 3-8258-7554-7

Jürgen Werbick
Von Gott sprechen an der Grenze zum Verstummen
Bd. 40, 2004, 368 S., 29,90 €, gb.,
ISBN 3-8258-7946-1

Martin Rohner
Glück und Erlösung
Konstellationen einer modernen Selbstverständigung
Bd. 41, 2004, 288 S., 24,90 €, br.,
ISBN 3-8258-7991-7

LIT Verlag Münster – Berlin – Hamburg – London – Wien
Grevener Str./Fresnostr. 2 48159 Münster
Tel.: 0251 – 62 032 22 – Fax: 0251 – 23 19 72
e-Mail: vertrieb@lit-verlag.de – http://www.lit-verlag.de